# SHIFTING SANDS

The Unravelling of the Old Order in the Middle East

# SHIFTING SANDS

Edited by Raja Shehadeh and Penny Johnson

**P**

**PROFILE BOOKS**

First published in Great Britain in 2015 by
PROFILE BOOKS LTD
3 Holford Yard
Bevin Way
London
WC1X 9HD
*www.profilebooks.com*

In association with the Edinburgh International Book Festival

A CIP catalogue record for this book is available from the British Library.

ISBN 978 1 78125 522 3
eISBN 978 1 78283 192 1

# CONTENTS

*In the Present Tense: The Unravelling of the Old Order*

*Living and Writing in the Middle East: Fiction, Imagination and History*

# THE SIGNIFICANCE OF A SCREWDRIVER

## Penny Johnson

*To Ra'ed Taysir al Hom, who defused bombs with a screwdriver until his luck ran out*

RA'ED AL HOM, the head of northern Gaza's only bomb disposal unit, died on 13 August 2014, the third day of a temporary ceasefire in Israel's war on Gaza and the second day of the five panels on the Middle East at the Edinburgh International Book Festival which inspired this book. Ra'ed, a resident of Gaza's Jabaliya refugee camp, was already a hero to Palestinians. With no protective clothing and little equipment, he had successfully defused 400 unexploded 'objects': ordnance dropped by the Israeli air force and army that hit homes, Gaza's crowded streets and, in one case, a bicycle repair shop. Arriving in Edinburgh from our home in Palestine and still shaken by the events taking place there, Raja and I were hit particularly hard by his death, which came while he was trying to defuse a 500-kilogram explosive. Defusing bombs with screwdrivers – this image haunted us as panellists travelled through a century of crisis and wars, colonial powers, new borders and fragile states, great cities and unending conquest, authoritarian power and people's civic resistance.

As the rain beat on the book festival tent, sometimes softly and sometimes with bullet-like intensity, reminding many of us of moments at home, fifteen writers – historians, novelists, social and cultural critics, travel and memoir writers – addressed large and enthusiastic audiences. Their presentations, like the essays in this book, were thoughtful, deeply informed and replete with observations that illuminate the present, past and future of the region. But they were not cold and dispassionate: the Middle East for some is home and family, for others a lost homeland or a beloved landscape of memory, but for all a place of friends and colleagues and the subject of a writer's insistent quest to understand. Thus noted historian Khaled Fahmy from Cairo began by reading the just-released Human Rights Watch Report on the Egyptian army's mass killing of protesters at Raba'a square in Cairo, on the anniversary of that event, and went on to probe a peasants' revolt in the nineteenth century to try to understand the deeper dynamics of Egypt and the Arab world today. Alev Scott held up a T-shirt she wore in the Gezi Park protests in Turkey in the summer of 2013, while offering a sober and sobering assessment of its aftermath. Tamim al-Barghouti provided a broad and innovative framework for understanding the dynamics of contemporary popular revolt against authoritarian Arab states – and also read part of his powerful poem that resonates with the Gaza War.

There are many ways the Middle East is defined and named: several United Nations organisations suggest the geographically correct but historically and politically weak 'Western Asia', while the World Bank and other international institutions prefer to talk of 'MENA', the Middle East and North Africa. Arabists – and indeed many Arabs – speak of the 'Arab world', dropping off Turkey, Iran and the non-Arab populations residing in Arab countries. Then there are those who simply speak of 'the region', perhaps the vaguest term but one that signals a place and people that are interconnected. While one would perhaps prefer the rich culinary connections as a guide to the region, today one defines 'the region' by serial crises and insecurity. A region on fire in far too many ways.

A pen is less useful than a screwdriver; a writer's task is certainly less pragmatic and exponentially less dangerous than bomb defusing, and Ra'ed al Hom's life and death are no metaphor. Yet the urgency of understanding the wave of events that terrible summer and onwards – indeed, the aftermath of the Arab Spring – from the war in Gaza to the advance of the Islamic State to the floods of Syrian and other refugees – brought writers together in Edinburgh armed only with a pen and a voice to probe the unravelling of the old order in the Middle East and its consequences.

That mission took us back a hundred years to the outbreak of the First World War.

:    :

One might think that urgent contemporary crises overwhelm historical events when it comes to reflecting on and writing about the Middle East. But, as our contributors show so eloquently, the events of a century ago are not simply background to today's conflagrations, but producers of the same. Consider an event that for many seemed to come out of the blue that summer: on 10 June, the Islamic State of Iraq and the Levant (ISIL, or Daesh in Arabic, or simply IS, the Islamic State) took over Mosul as the Iraqi army literally evaporated, a military defeat called by veteran journalist Patrick Cockburn 'one of great military debacles in history'.[1] Unlike the measured on-the-ground analyses of Cockburn and some fellow journalists, politicians and pundits outside the region rushed in with little information but many generalisations about the Islamic State and its trajectory. What can a long view tell us?

In his essay, James Barr takes us back to 1915, as two men, Mark Sykes, a 36-year-old English Tory politician, and François Georges-Picot, a French diplomat, sit down over a map and draw a line in the sand, 'from the "e" of Acre [Palestine] to the last "k" in Kirkuk [Iraq]', dividing much of the region – particularly the Arab lands of the dying Ottoman Empire – into French and British spheres of influence, later regularised as Mandates. The ensuing 1916 secret agreement, as Barr argues convincingly (and with telling anecdotes), signalled an immense change in the political

4

geography of the Middle East. Thus today, while 'erasing' the border between Syria and Iraq through military conquest, the Islamic State declared the end of the Sykes–Picot Agreement and a new caliphate in June 2014. Surely, as William Faulkner told us, 'The past is never dead. It's not even past.' We would argue, however, that the militants of ISIL are poor historians, seemingly intent on erasing not just the last hundred years, but thirteen centuries of Islamic and Middle Eastern civilisation. As Justin Marozzi reminds us in his own long view from Baghdad, 'For the first time in 2,000 years the ancient city of Mosul has no Christians.' Both in ISIL's erasure of the past and its utilisation of an Islamic essence that defies history, we can recall the Khmer Rouge, in an apt comparison by political analyst Mouin Rabbani,[2] who also argues convincingly that ISIL is a thoroughly modernist project. Its savvy and cruel use of media also attests that it is a creature of our troubled twenty-first century.

Avi Shlaim points to the Sykes–Picot Agreement as one of the three contradictory promises made by the British and examines the other two, the Hussein–McMahon correspondence, pledging British support for an independent Arab nation if the Arabs entered the war on the Allied side and the Balfour Declaration, promising a homeland in Palestine for the Jewish people. The Balfour Declaration is a staple in the recitation of the bitter history of the conflict between Palestine and Israel, but Shlaim widens the lens and makes a provocative new argument in his essay, calling it 'one of the most colossal blunders in British imperial history'.

Salim Tamari brings us face to face with the terrible consequences of the First World War in the eastern Mediterranean on the ground, where about a sixth of the population of Greater Syria died from war, famine and disease. Through the memoirs of civilians and the diaries of three Ottoman soldiers, he traces the ruptures in identity, and in particular new assertions of local and national identity. Tamari notes that reversions to local identity can be discovered 'in the war and devastation that are happening today'.

Indeed, what Avi Shlaim calls the 'post-Ottoman syndrome' has also had long-lasting consequences, which he identifies as 'turmoil, instability and a deficit of rights for the peoples of the region', all much in evidence today. The lack of legitimacy Shlaim describes in some post-war states (his example, tellingly, is Iraq) surfaces as a deep cause for popular rebellion in Khaled Fahmy's analysis of Egypt. Fahmy, one of the many thousands of Egyptians at Tahrir Square in January 2011, asks the probing question 'Why were we demonstrating?' He reflects on the lack of constitutional and political rights, but then goes on to ask, 'Were we protesting against the very nature of the modern Egyptian state?'

Here, Fahmy's searching question reminds us of a key aspect of the writer's job, namely (to liberally paraphrase Chekhov) to ask the right questions rather than to provide pat answers. And understanding the failures of what Tamim al-Barghouti calls the 'cracked cauldrons' of the 'colonially created Arab states' takes us beyond Egypt as well. Al-Barghouti's searing critique begins with the failure to perform the functions 'for which humans invented states in the first place': to protect and defend their citizens from civil war and invasion. Ramita Navai on Iran and Alev Scott on Turkey remind us that crises in state–society relations in the Middle East are not confined to Arab states, but take on other dimensions in these two seemingly more stable, and increasingly more crucial, political and social environments.

Nowhere are the failures of state responsibility to society more acute than in Syria, and nowhere perhaps is the writer's responsibility to ask the right questions more pressing or to avoid pat answers more appropriate. Indeed, finding words to describe the dangers ordinary Syrians face – with 200,000 dead, at least 2 million refugees and half the population displaced as of February 2015 – is itself a daunting task. And it is both ordinary Syrians struggling to survive and extraordinary Syrians continuing to create and advocate for their people who are addressed by our three contributors writing about Syria. Robin Yassin-Kassab visited northern Syria to hold workshops with refugee children in 2011 and 2012 and observes, 'Neither visit took me to a country or a people recognisable from the Western media.' Yassin-Kassab's passionate polemic on the failures of his own UK government and people to aid the Syrian opposition has a quiet counterpoint in his encounters with 'human beings in transformation', debating and discussing everything with deep commitment and bracing humour. That many of these activists (and armed militants as well) of the non-sectarian opposition are currently trapped 'between two states' – the Baathist and the Islamic – between the brutality of the Syrian regime and the encroaching horrors of ISIL, provides a telling and tragic image of Syria today. Malu Halasa provides a much-needed breath of optimism in her engaging and important discussion of 'perhaps the only positive development in over four years of brutal conflict', a cultural revolution with activists across the country (and now abroad) producing posters, cartoons, videos, comic strips, rap and other forms of street art that mobilise, boost morale, give direction to protest and advocate globally via social media for rights, life and democracy for the Syrian people. Dawn Chatty discusses 'what you don't read' about the Syrian crisis and argues that in multi-ethnic Syria communities continue to cohere and find resilience in older, local identities. In particular, she notes the emergence of Bedouin tribes and Kurds as possible major players and argues, 'The lines drawn on the map of the Levant by Sir Mark Sykes may no longer hold, but the pre-existing social and cultural groups of the Levant with their multitude of ethno-religious belongings will remain.' This long view situates Syria in local, regional and Western histories, rather than in a 'black hole' that defies understanding.

The tendency to view Western and Middle Eastern histories as separate, or at least to include Western

nations in the history of the Middle East only as colonial powers, has often led to seeing the entire Middle
East as a black hole – whether not ready for democracy,
doomed to eternal authoritarianism, defined by Islam
or, in its most neoconservative version, as an exporter of
only hatred and terror. While paying close attention to
regional, national and local histories, our contributors
can also be usefully read as providing ways of understanding global dynamics that affect us all. The crises
in the Middle East are a lens to understand present
and coming crises in a global order that increasingly
produces inequalities and concentrations of economic
and political power. The separation of power and people
which marks our age may produce crises in the nation-
state, a turn to religious and exclusive identities, or
political and social rebellion at great odds – all features
of the current conflagrations in the Middle East.

The earthquake of the Arab Spring in Tunisia and
Egypt in 2011 delivered the first crack to Middle East
exceptionalism, where the Arab world was no longer
the province of long-living dictators, oil monarchies
and armies but of people demanding dignity and
change. In what the ubiquitous Slovenian philosopher
Slavoj Žižek called the 'year of dreaming dangerously',
Tahrir Square and Tunis were linked with Occupy
Wall Street, protests in Greece and the Indignados
in Spain. Žižek, always the Hegelian, also observed
that the emancipatory dreams of these protesters
were shadowed by the destructive dreams propelling
Breivik [the Norwegian who murdered seventy-seven

people, mostly teenagers, on the island of Utøya in the summer of 2011] and racist and anti-immigrant populists across Europe,[3] an early warning that the wider world, not just the Middle East, is on dangerous ground. Tamim al-Barghouti describes a regional terrain that has global resonance: where 'narratives are replacing structures' and 'ideas, for better or for worse, are replacing leaders', noting that these new forms of political mobilisation characterise the liberatory moment of Tahrir Square – but also, in societies with ethnic or sectarian divisions, can be exploited.

'How did the Arab Spring morph into an Arab nightmare?' asked Khaled Fahmy. He gives no sound-bite answer, but instead probes five 'deep problems' that need to be both understood and addressed in an extended process of change. These range from the scourge of petro-dollars to deeper existential questions on the role of religion in politics and what I would interpret from his remarks as the search for a usable past to inform a better future. And he offers in his own prediction for the future an intangible resource: hope.

Hope may seem a scant commodity in today's crisis-ridden landscape. Indeed, for three of our contributors discussing living and writing in the Middle East, and in particular the writing of fiction, hope is located in the imagination. Kuwaiti writer and scholar Mai al-Nakib notes that fiction can draw 'attention away from a dominant order that often seems to choke off any sense of possibility'. Reclaiming the cosmopolitanism of Kuwait's past through the fictional imagination counters a 'state of amnesia' where, for example, the 380,000 Palestinians who lived in Kuwait until 1991 have been erased in the present normative version of the past. Marilyn Booth finds that 'fiction's histories', whether in the contemporary writing of al-Nakib and Selma Dabbagh, or the novels of Arab women writers of a hundred years ago, offer a 'critical, alternative history of communities', as well as reminding us of the persistence of issues of social equality and youthful aspirations. Dabbagh embraced the challenges of a diaspora writer imagining a 'fictional Gaza' and in so doing not only brought Gaza into her readers' imaginations, but healed a rift in Palestinian lives.

In her essay, Selma Dabbagh also discusses some of the obstacles faced by writers in Arabic – from lack of translation and resources to censorship in their home countries – and adds a personal note as a British-Palestinian novelist writing in English. To her observation that book buyers often classify literature from the Middle East as necessarily dark and gloomy and thus unmarketable, we might add a note, from trawling the blogosphere or indeed reviewing almost any newspaper comments page or articles about Palestine and Israel or Islam, that the issues are not only already known, but occasion instant and often vitriolic and industrially produced responses. There is thus a need for other spaces and forms of engagements – offered, we hope, by this and many other books on the Middle East that do not provide instant answers but engage readers in exploring the questions.

The writers in *Shifting Sands* are not aiming to inform readers about the very latest events – which will be superseded in any case by the time of publication – but to provide ways to understand these events. Nor do the writers aim to produce a uniform analysis – some may indeed disagree – but rather to explore the major themes and issues in the unravelling of a century-old order in the Middle East. The passionate civility of audiences at the Edinburgh International Book Festival and their probing questions contributed to this book and we thank the Festival for providing the opportunity for this engagement, away from the overheated world of information that can impede a deeper understanding.

⋮ ⋮

In the afterword, Raja Shehadeh, through an exploration of conversations in a shared taxi ride from Ramallah to Jerusalem, illuminates the dilemmas of the present dark times. He argues, however, that a solution to the Palestine/Israel problem, based on equality and an end to exclusion, can offer a new vision for the Middle East based on cooperation and cosmopolitanism.

This vision may seem distant amid the present conflagrations. Our summer of fire in 2014 ushered in a violent autumn and winter in the Middle East. The Gaza War was (perhaps) over, but the plight of Gazans remained unaddressed, while the wars in Syria and Iraq escalated with terrible consequences for civilians.

However, we also marked another anniversary, the twenty-fifth anniversary of the fall of the Berlin Wall on 9 November 2014. Like the Arab Spring and other utopian moments, the euphoria at this signal event did not lead to a more peaceful and equal global order. Instead, we are plagued by rampant social inequality, unregulated economic growth with its disastrous environmental consequences, and what the poet Robert Lowell called 'small war after small war until the end of time'. The world may no longer embrace MAD (Mutual Assured Destruction), but it is increasingly dangerous.

With the perilous situation in much of the Middle East today, we cannot afford false optimism, and the writers in *Shifting Sands* do not shy away from hard, sometimes painful, analysis. But we also cannot afford to ignore what Alev Scott calls 'civic courage', that intangible but vital resource. On the anniversary of the fall of the Berlin Wall, young Palestinian activists in the West Bank gathered and, using hammers and their hands, smashed a hole in what Palestinians call the 'Apartheid Wall'. And in the village of Battir in the southern West Bank – now a UNESCO World Heritage site because of its ancient terraced hills – children flew white balloons over the railway station where trains no longer stop on their way to the coast, across the Wall they are forbidden to traverse, with messages against occupation and for peace. 'From Battir to Berlin' was the village's message. Balloons and hammers: other versions of the screwdriver against bombs that generate a fragile hope.

# LINES IN THE SAND

**The Great War and the Remaking of the Middle East**

# THE POST-OTTOMAN SYNDROME

## Avi Shlaim

MUCH OF THE MIDDLE EAST has been living with a chronic condition for almost a century which I term the post-Ottoman syndrome. Its symptoms are turmoil, instability and a deficit of rights for the peoples of the region. A major cause is the lack of legitimacy of the new political and territorial order that emerged in the wake of the First World War and the collapse of the Ottoman Empire. That state system, in the lands formerly controlled by the Ottomans, was largely the creation of colonial powers and designed to serve their interests.

In the course of the First World War, the Entente powers, Britain and France, made various secret plans for dividing the lands of the Ottoman Empire in the event of victory. Behind France's back, Britain promised a share of the spoils to its Arab allies to induce them to take up arms against their Ottoman overlords. Towards the end of the war Britain made public promises to support the Zionist project in Palestine which were incompatible with its earlier undertakings. To make sense of the tangled and tortuous diplomacy behind these contradictory promises, it is therefore necessary to examine not only the relations between the two colonial powers but also their relations with their respective local allies.

Wartime diplomacy was further complicated by mutual mistrust between the two colonial powers. The French called Britain 'perfidious Albion', based on its long record of deviousness and double-dealing. Britain did indeed act in a selfish manner, but there was nothing unusual in that: selfishness is in the DNA of colonial powers. France too was not exactly a paragon of virtue. My aim here is not to dwell on wartime diplomacy, fascinating as it is, but to spell out its consequences for the post-war regional order. My main emphasis will be on the borders set by the colonial powers and on the successor states they created after the fall of the Ottoman Empire. To be sure, wartime partition plans were rather like drawing 'lines in the sand'. The bargaining power of each of the participants kept changing in line with its fluctuating fortunes on the battlefield. But the international borders that the victors set after the war have lasted down to the present day, with the exception of Israel–Palestine. They have proved to be remarkably stable, almost sacrosanct – perhaps the only stable element in a volatile region. The way in which these borders emerged is therefore not merely of historical interest; it is a crucial element in the remaking of the modern Middle East.

In the course of searching for allies against the Ottoman Turks, the British made a number of promises, some of them secret and some open. The three most important promises were to the Arabs, the French and the Jews. First, in an effort to foster an anti-Turkish rebellion in the Arab lands, Britain entered into secret negotiations with Hussein, the Sharif of Mecca, whose descendants later became the kings of Jordan. The Hashemites claimed direct descent from the Prophet Muhammad and were hereditary guardians of the Holy Places in Mecca and Medina in their ancestral home in the Hijaz in Western Arabia, but they were also nominal vassals of the Ottoman Sultan. Conspiring with infidels against a Muslim overlord was quite a risky undertaking for the conservative Sharif, hence the need for secrecy. Between July 1915 and March 1916 ten letters were exchanged between the Sharif and Sir Henry McMahon, the British high commissioner in Egypt. In these letters Britain promised the Sharif to recognise and support an independent Arab kingdom under his leadership after the war in return for taking up arms against the Ottomans. The British promise was vaguely worded, imprecise about borders and failed to make clear whether Palestine was to be included in the Arab kingdom.

Vague as they were, Britain's assurances led to the outbreak of the Arab Revolt against the Turks in June 1916. As its origins make all too clear, the Arab Revolt, which is remembered to this day as the golden age of Arab nationalism, was in essence an Anglo-Hashemite plot, an unholy alliance against the Ottoman Sublime Porte. Britain financed the Arab Revolt as well as supplying arms, provisions, artillery support and experts in desert warfare, among whom was the legendary T. E. Lawrence, better known as 'Lawrence of Arabia'. The Hashemites promised much more than they were able to deliver, and the military value of the revolt was modest; indeed, Lawrence's account greatly exaggerated its military successes.[1]

Second, Britain reached a secret understanding with France in May 1916, the Sykes–Picot Agreement, discussed by James Barr in this volume and covered in fascinating detail in his book *A Line in the Sand* (2011). The two officials drafted a plan to divide the land between the Mediterranean and the Persian Gulf into two 'spheres of influence' in the event of victory. No agreement could be reached on Palestine, so the compromise solution was to place it under an international regime.

Future historians would cite the Sykes–Picot Agreement as a prime example of imperial perfidy. Palestinian historian George Antonius denounced it as 'a shocking document' and 'a startling piece of double-dealing'.[2] The perfidy is undeniable, but its consequences have often been exaggerated. It is a common misconception – shared by, among others, the Islamic State today – to think that the Sykes–Picot Agreement fixed the borders of the modern Middle East. In fact, it bears little resemblance to the borders that were settled by the League of Nations at the conference of

San Remo in 1920. Instead, Sykes–Picot is significant as the beginning of the process of colonial division of the region.

The third and most famous British undertaking, again vaguely worded and imprecise but this time not secret, was the promise contained in the Balfour Declaration of 2 November 1917 to support the establishment of a national home for the Jewish people in Palestine. At that time the Jews made up barely 10 per cent of the population of Palestine. Supporting their national rights in Palestine meant denying them to the Arab majority. Balfour's declaration was thus a classic colonial document. The main motive behind it was less to support the fledgling Zionist movement than to harness the perceived influence of world Jewry to the British war effort. The prime mover behind the declaration was David Lloyd George, who became prime minister in December 1916. His support for Zionism was based on a huge overestimate of Jewish influence. In aligning Britain with the Zionist movement, he acted in the mistaken – and anti-Semitic – view that the Jews turned the wheels of history. In fact, the Jewish people had little influence other than the myth of clandestine power. Issuing the Balfour Declaration turned out to be one of the most colossal blunders in British imperial history. It brought Britain much ill will in the Arab world and no corresponding benefits, not even the gratitude of its Jewish protégés.

British policymakers had no clear idea as to how they would reconcile the promises they made to the

Arabs, the French and the Zionists. Consequently, there was confusion as well as duplicity in Britain's policy towards its wartime allies. Furthermore, as the war progressed, the British policymakers became more acquisitive. Lenin said that imperialism causes war. In Britain's case, it was the war that fuelled imperialism. Lloyd George wanted to grab more and more Ottoman territory, regardless of the agreements entered into by his predecessors. His aim was to establish British hegemony in the Middle East, to gain access to its oil fields and to bring Palestine into the British sphere of influence.

Lloyd George's imperial ambitions in the Middle East went against the current of American anti-colonialism, which was running high with Woodrow Wilson as president. The President's high-minded attitude to politics, enunciated in his Fourteen Points, denounced secret diplomacy and upheld the right of small nations to self-determination. America entered the war in April 1917, a month after the Bolshevik revolution put Russia *hors de combat*, and there was a short period of intense involvement in the affairs of the Middle East before lapsing once again into isolation. Woodrow Wilson knew that the European powers had entered into secret agreements to aggrandise their empires and he did not want his country to be associated with a war that served imperial interests. He wanted a war to end all wars by basing the post-war order on the right to national self-determination. Naturally, some Middle Easterners associated Wilson's Fourteen Points with their own aspiration to achieve freedom from European domination and welcomed the arrival of the anti-imperialist power as a participant in Middle East politics.

Feeling on the defensive, Britain and France issued a joint declaration on 7 November 1918, a few days before the Armistice, in which they clearly recognised the Arab right to self-determination. The declaration opened with a statement of breathtaking insincerity:

> The end which France and Great Britain have in
> view in their prosecution in the East of the war
> let loose by German ambition is the complete
> and definitive liberation of the peoples so long
> oppressed by the Turks and the establishment
> of national Governments and Administrations
> drawing their authority from the initiative and
> free choice of indigenous populations.

It ended on a self-righteous note, denying any wish to impose their own system, promising to respect the will of the people and to secure impartial and equal justice for all.

One searches in vain for any trace of these lofty ideals in the conduct of the European statesmen at the peace conference that convened in Paris in January 1919. It was not the rights of small nations but the rivalries and clashes of the big powers that dominated proceedings. Lloyd George wanted to bring America into the Middle East as Britain's ally and even suggested that America should have responsibility for

Constantinople and Armenia, which had originally been assigned to tsarist Russia. Wilson, however, resisted all of the arrangements proposed by the European powers, suggesting instead an investigating commission to ascertain the desires of the people in the area. The clash between Lloyd George's old-fashioned imperialism and Woodrow Wilson's ineffectual idealism ensured that the peace negotiations went from bad to worse.

The Arabs were represented at the peace conference by Emir Faisal, Sharif Hussein's son, who had formed a temporary administration in Syria but was out of his depth in the world of European diplomacy and eventually left Paris empty-handed. Faisal and his nationalist followers pinned their hopes on American help in their struggle for independence. These hopes were strongly articulated in the resolutions of the General Syrian Congress, which assembled in Damascus on 2 July 1919. 'We rely,' said the delegates, 'on President Wilson's declaration that his object in entering the War was to put an end to acquisitive designs for imperialistic purposes.' They demanded the repudiation of the Sykes–Picot Agreement and the Balfour Declaration; the recognition of Syria, including Palestine, as a sovereign state with Emir Faisal as king; and the granting of independence to Iraq. In conclusion, the delegates affirmed their belief that the settlement should reflect the real wishes of the people and looked to 'President Wilson and the liberal American nation, who are known for their sincere and generous sympathy with

the aspirations of weak nations, for help in the fulfilment of our hopes'.

President Wilson did try to help by sending to
Palestine and Syria a commission of inquiry to find
out the wishes of the inhabitants. But the King–Crane
Commission was a purely American affair, since France
and Britain declined to participate in this exercise.
The commissioners reported general opposition to
Zionism and to the imposition of a French mandate.
They also made recommendations for Syria, Palestine and Iraq that were designed to lead to independence at the earliest possible date. But the work of the
commission was an exercise in futility. What Woodrow
Wilson failed to understand was that consultation is a
purely academic exercise — academic in the sense of
futile — unless the consulting body has the authority
and the will to act on what it learns.

By the end of 1919 Woodrow Wilson had had
enough of what he described as 'the whole disgusting
scramble' and sailed back to the United States, turning
over his Arab admirers to the tender mercies of the
colonial powers. When the high-sounding Supreme
Council of the Peace Conference met in San Remo
in April 1920, it brushed aside all Arab claims and
the wishes of the inhabitants and reached a settlement
that satisfied only the victors. It was fundamentally a
victors' peace. Britain received a League of Nations
mandate for Iraq and Palestine which included Transjordan. France received a mandate for Syria and the
Lebanon. Mandates were imperialism by other means.

In Arab eyes the San Remo decisions were nothing but a betrayal and a profound humiliation. They sealed the fate of the United Kingdom of Syria, which had been proclaimed by the Greater Syrian Congress on 7 March 1920, with Faisal on the throne. In July 1920 French forces marched on Damascus, banished Faisal into exile and took over the government of the country. Thus was created the modern state of Syria, under French control and on the ruins of the dream of a united and independent Arab kingdom led by the Hashemites.

The French were no friends of Arab nationalism, viewing the Arab Revolt as Britain in Arab headgear. France's traditional friends were the different Christian sects, and especially the Maronites, who formed the large majority of the population in Mount Lebanon, and on 31 August 1920 the French created yet another state with new borders, issuing a decree establishing the state of Greater Lebanon.

The settlement imposed on the Arab countries by the allies provoked deep resentment throughout the region and this expressed itself in acts of defiance and violence: 1920 saw trouble in Egypt, serious disturbances in Syria, riots in Palestine and a full-scale uprising in Iraq. All these rebellions had their roots not in a sinister Bolshevik conspiracy, as many Britons believed at the time, but in a local dislike of foreigners and foreign domination, buttressed by Muslim resistance to having Christian powers rule over them. Britain's instinctive reaction as an imperial power was to stamp out the violence, but it was also realised that the lid could not be kept indefinitely on the Middle East cauldron by military repression pure and simple.

The task of formulating a policy fell to Winston Churchill when he became Colonial Secretary in February 1919. His principal adviser was T. E. Lawrence, an advocate of indirect rule or enlightened imperialism. It was under Lawrence's influence that Churchill adopted the 'Sharifian' plan of dividing the British sphere of influence into a number of states to be headed by the Sharif of Mecca and his sons. Lawrence pressed hardest the claims of Emir Faisal. The Sharifian plan went some way towards mitigating Britain's sense of guilt for letting down the Sharif, but it had two other, more practical, merits to recommend it. First, as Lawrence pointed out, as imported rulers lacking a power base of their own, the Hashemites would be dependent on Britain. Second, as Churchill pointed out, because they were a family, Britain would be able to play them off against one another to attain its own ends.

The first step in implementing this Sharifian plan was to offer Faisal the throne of Iraq. The invention of the Iraqi throne provided a neat solution to Britain's own problem of carrying a spare prince. It also entailed a handsome consolation prize to the prince in question for the throne he had lost in Damascus. Faisal's ascent to the throne in Baghdad was carefully stage-managed by Sir Percy Cox, the high commissioner for Iraq, and his assistant Gertrude Bell, whose obsession with the

Hashemites and passion for king-making matched that of Lawrence. Other candidates were persuaded to withdraw, while Sayyid Talib, who proclaimed the slogan 'Iraq for the Iraqis', was arrested and deported. The remaining opposition to Faisal, mostly from the Kurds and the Shiites, was neutralised. A referendum was then arranged to give Britain's candidate a veneer of popular legitimacy. Ninety-six per cent of Iraqis, it was claimed, wanted Faisal as their king, and he duly ascended the throne on 23 August 1921. As one critic of British policy noted, the 1921 settlement had two notable results: first, it introduced anti-British senti- ment as a fundamental principle of Iraqi politics and, second, 'it justified and sanctioned violent and arbi- trary proceedings and built them into the structure of Iraqi politics'.[3]

Equally arbitrary and equally calculated to suit Brit- ain's own political, strategic and commercial interests was the delineation of Iraq's borders. These took little account of the divisions within Iraq along linguistic or religious lines into Kurds in the north, Sunni Muslims in the centre and Shiite Muslims in the south. The logic behind the enterprise was not easy to fathom. To one observer it seemed that 'Iraq was created by Churchill, who had the mad idea of joining two widely separated oil wells, Kirkuk and Mosul, by uniting three widely separated peoples: the Kurds, the Sunnis and the Shiites.'[4]

The second stage in the execution of the Shari- fian plan was to let Faisal's elder brother, Abdullah, rule over the vacant lot which the British christened, if that is the right word, the Emirate of Transjordan, bolstered by financial assistance from Britain. A statement was issued excluding Transjordan from the provisions for a Jewish national home, which initially applied to the whole area of the Palestine mandate. Churchill was well satisfied with his handiwork and frequently boasted that he had created the Emirate of Transjordan by the stroke of his pen one bright Sunday afternoon and still had time to paint the magnificent views of Jerusalem.

The fiercest Arab hostility towards Britain was provoked by the latter's policy in Palestine. On 1 July 1921 Britain set up a civil administration headed by a high commissioner to govern the country directly. The promise to support a national home for the Jewish people contained in the Balfour Declaration was incorporated into the terms of the League of Nations mandate. At the time of the Balfour Declaration the Jews constituted less than 10 per cent of the population of the country. So from the very start a tragic contradiction was built into the mandate: Britain could only meet its obligations to the Jews by denying to the Arab majority their natural right to self-determination. Palestine was to be the exception to the universally valid rule that a territory belongs to the majority of the people who live there.

Moreover, the enthusiasm with which Britain embraced the Zionist cause in 1917 had largely evaporated by the early 1920s. The conflicting promises, statements and declarations made by the allies regarding Palestine created a smokescreen of almost impenetrable density. One of the very few honest remarks on the subject was made in retrospect by the author of the Balfour Declaration. 'In short, so far as Palestine is concerned,' wrote Balfour, 'the Powers have made no statement of fact which is not admittedly wrong, and no declaration of policy which, at least in the letter, they have not always intended to violate.'[5]

In the conduct of negotiations over borders, British representatives were capable of acting in a most arbitrary and autocratic manner to further Britain's imperial interests. During the negotiations in 1922 to define the frontiers of Iraq, Kuwait and the Najd (the forerunner of present-day Saudi Arabia), for example, Sir Percy Cox reprimanded Abd al-Aziz ibn al-Rahman al Faisal al Saud, the mighty Sultan of the Najd, like a naughty schoolboy and reduced him to tears. Ibn Saud was forced to yield land to Iraq but was later compensated at the expense of Kuwait. The borders imposed by Cox, who was known to the Arabs as Kokkus, deliberately restricted Iraq's access to the Persian Gulf. These borders did not fully satisfy any of the parties, least of all Iraq, which felt it was entitled to the whole of Kuwait. They therefore continued to generate friction and instability.

What was left of the Ottoman Empire after the allies had nearly finished carving it up became the modern state of Turkey. The collapse of empires invariably has consequences for international order and so it was in this case. The Ottoman Empire had provided a political system that was far from perfect, but it worked. During the First World War Britain and France destroyed the old order in the Arabic-speaking Middle East, but they did not spare much thought for the long-term consequences of their actions. In the aftermath of the war they built a new political and territorial order in the region on the ruins of the old order. They refashioned the Middle East in their own image. They created states, they nominated persons to govern them and they laid down frontiers between them. But the new states, for the most part, were small and unstable and the rulers lacked legitimacy, while the frontiers were arbitrary, illogical and unjust, giving rise to powerful irredentist tendencies.

The new order settled Europe's century-long Eastern Question: who and what would succeed the Ottomans? But it also raised a new Middle Eastern Question within the Middle East itself, and that was whether the people of the region would accept the new state system, which was based on European ideas, European interests and European management. Would they be able and, if so, would they be willing to operate by the new ground rules? The answer is that powerful local forces, both secular and religious, rejected the new state system and the ground rules that went with it. Indeed, it has been this absence of legitimacy that has been a central feature of Middle East politics ever since the old order was blown away.

To Arab nationalists the new order meant betrayal

by the allies of their wartime promises, military occupation, the division of the area into spheres of influence and exploitation of its raw materials. Hostility towards the authors of the new order was further fuelled by what they saw as the planting in Palestine, in the heart of the Arab world, of a dangerous imperialist bridgehead in the form of the Jewish national home.

In short, the post-war order imposed by the Entente powers created a belt of turmoil and instability stretching from the Mediterranean to the Persian Gulf. Its key feature was lack of legitimacy. This situation may be termed the post-Ottoman syndrome. It laid the groundwork for conflicts that continue to plague the region. In this sense the Paris peace settlement is not just a chapter in history, or past history as Americans are apt to say. It is the story of our own times. It lies at the root of the turmoil and instability, countless territorial disputes, struggles for national liberation, rebellions and revolutions, civil wars and interstate wars that have become such familiar features of the international politics of the Middle East in the post-Second World War era. The post-1918 peace settlement is at the very heart of the current conflicts between the Arabs and Israel, between Arabs and other Arabs, between some Arabs and the West. Field Marshal Archibald Percival Wavell, 1st Earl Wavell, who served in the Palestine campaign during the First World War, summed it up in one line: 'After "the war to end war" they seem to have been pretty successful in Paris at making a "Peace to end Peace".'[6]

# THE DIVISIVE LINE: THE BIRTH AND LONG LIFE OF THE SYKES–PICOT AGREEMENT

## James Barr

THE SYKES–PICOT AGREEMENT came crashing back into the headlines in the summer of 2014 after a propaganda video shot by the Islamic State showed a bulldozer carving a passage through the sandbank that delineates the Syria–Iraq border. It was certainly a graphic illustration of how the jihadi group had become a transnational phenomenon that controlled the vacuum left by the failing Syrian and Iraqi states. But the Islamic State propagandists tried to vest it with greater symbolism. It was the 'end of Sykes–Picot,' they claimed, in a reference to the wartime deal whereby Britain and France carved up the Middle East between them.

Cue many articles about the 98-year-old Sykes–Picot Agreement, and fierce debate about whether, as Osama bin Laden liked to claim, it can be blamed for Arab woes, or not. Some, pointing to the colonial legacy, said it was responsible; others retorted that the difference between the Sykes–Picot partition and the

*The map of the 1916 Sykes-Picot agreement divided
the Middle East with a diagonal line that ran from the
Mediterranean to the Persian frontier. France would rule
Zone A and the adjacent northern area; Britain Zone
B and the adjacent southern area. The two men signed
the bottom right corner. (British National Archives)*

current political map, or the more recent failings of the
states themselves, meant that it wasn't. The truth lies
somewhere in between.

The idea that the deal would still be so controversial would surely have surprised one of the two men
involved in its creation, eighteen months into the First
World War. Sir Mark Sykes was thirty-six years old

when he hurried into Downing Street on the morning of 16 December 1915, clutching a handful of notes, a square War Office map and an expedient proposal that was designed to address French fears about the awkward Eastern Question: what would happen to the Middle East if Britain and France emerged as victors?

It was ironic that Sykes's idea would change the Middle East for ever, because the discussion that followed was only superficially about the region. Fundamentally – and this is what made dealing with the issue so urgent – it was about addressing a disagreement that looked as if it might tear Britain's alliance with France apart.

By December 1915, eighteen months into a war that some had predicted would be over by the previous Christmas, the Anglo-French Entente Cordiale was under severe strain. There had always had been disagreement over strategy. The French were adamant that a great offensive on the western front was urgently required to drive the Germans from their soil. The British argued for delay while they recruited a vast army of volunteers and reorganised their war effort, for, too often, their troops went into battle without enough ammunition. The consequence, in the short run, was that in the first year of the war the French did most of the fighting and took most of the casualties. Disagreement became distrust. A fortnight before Sykes's meeting in Downing Street the British ambassador in Paris had been forced to admit (after months of denials) that he was beginning to hear the view among his contacts that 'we are making use of France against Germany for our own sole benefit and that much greater sacrifices are being made by France'.[1]

Events in the Middle East during 1915 had strengthened these misgivings. When the early French offensives failed, a faction within the British government, led by Kitchener and Churchill, proposed a rethink. Looking east, they argued that the defeat of Germany's decrepit Ottoman allies would break the deadlock by opening a new front in south-east Europe to which the Germans would have to send troops.

There was another reason why the British wished to deal swiftly with the Ottomans. This was to end the threat of a jihad. After the Ottoman Empire joined the war on the Germans' side, its Sultan had declared a holy war against his enemies. Jumpy British officials had watched ever since for signs that the British Empire's 100 million Muslim subjects might rise up in answer to his call. They knew that the war could only be won in Europe, but feared it might be lost if British troops had to be diverted to fight rebellions in Egypt and India.

The French never shared the British neurosis about the jihad. Their scepticism about the British war plan turned into suspicion when they saw its details. Originally, the British had intended to grab the Ottoman Empire by its throat and kick it in the guts simultaneously through landings both on the Gallipoli peninsula and at the port of Alexandretta – modern Iskanderun – in the eastern corner of the Mediterranean where

Syria and Turkey meet and the railway that formed the backbone of Ottoman communications ran near the coast. The French had long entertained hopes of establishing a foothold in the eastern Mediterranean, and suspected that the Alexandretta landings were as much a British effort to thwart this dream as they were about winning the war. They were right to do so, because as Lawrence of Arabia, then working as an intelligence officer in Cairo, admitted at the time, 'The only place from which a fleet can operate against Egypt is Alexandretta.'[2] After the French vetoed this part of the plan, only the Gallipoli landings went ahead.

The wrangling over Alexandretta revealed old tensions that are worth explaining, because their recurrence added to the sense of malaise afflicting the Entente and triggered the Sykes–Picot Agreement. Britain and France had been rivals in the Middle East since the Napoleonic era. They were battling at this point not for its oil wealth – that would come later – but in the belief that control of Egypt in particular was a prerequisite for domination of the real prize: India.

The Anglo-French struggle had intensified in the second half of the nineteenth century following the completion of the Suez Canal and as the Ottoman Empire began to crumble. In 1875, when bankruptcy beckoned for the Egyptian ruler, Ismail (who was an Ottoman client), the British bought his stake in the canal to prevent the French (the other shareholder) from establishing a monopoly. When the Ottoman government's default the following year left British investors badly burned, the French rushed in to replace them, becoming the largest holders of Ottoman government bonds.

The Ottoman default prompted the British to think the unthinkable and abandon their previous policy of propping up the Ottomans. That led them to take over Cyprus in 1878 and Egypt in 1882. When the British then lost control of the Sudan after the murder of General Gordon, the French tried to exploit the vacuum. In 1895 they launched an expedition to claim, and dam, the headwaters of the Nile in an attempt to render Egypt, downstream, uninhabitable. Churchill, then a journalist, dismissed it as an attempt by 'eight French adventurers' to claim a territory that was 'twice the size of France'. But outlandish as it seemed, the threat was plausible enough to precipitate Kitchener's reconquest of the Sudan and the subsequent confrontation between his forces and the French in 1898 at Fashoda – the flyblown spot where France had raised the tricolore and was then forced to lower it in defeat. Today, the Fashoda Incident's nineteenth-century date makes it seem desperately remote, but to gain a sense of how recent it felt in 1915, you only have to imagine that Britain had almost gone to war with France in 1998.

Old habits died hard. As the plans to invade the Gallipoli peninsula were finalised, the British government anticipated victory and an argument with its allies over the division of the spoils. It set up a committee – what else? – to ensure that Britain's overriding priority, the security of India, was not simply preserved but reinforced. Sykes, a new Member of Parliament who was Kitchener's assistant, was the most junior member of this body.

Sykes possessed an engaging sense of humour and a flyaway imagination but he was not what we would call a 'details man'. He came from a landed Yorkshire family, an only child who had inherited the baronetcy from his late father, Sir Tatton, an odd man whose chief passions were church architecture, milk pudding and the maintenance of his body at a constant temperature. It was presumably in pursuit of the first of these that Sir Tatton had taken him on holiday to the Middle East in 1890.

Sykes was neither the first person nor the last to be entranced by the sense of going back in time, and he returned to the region repeatedly. When he joined the committee considering the future of the Ottoman Empire in early 1915 he had just published an entertainingly jaundiced history-cum-travel memoir that showed a visceral dislike of creeping modernity, yet sealed his reputation in political circles as an expert on the region. As one reviewer remarked, 'The facts which he has collected will be of the highest value when the settlement of the Eastern question comes to be undertaken.'[3]

In the committee's early discussions Sykes advocated splitting the region with the French, but his colleagues disagreed. In their view the best way to keep other powers away from India was to turn the existing Ottoman provinces into semi-independent states which Britain would seek to influence but not directly govern. Sykes was sent on a trip to Cairo and Delhi in the summer to canvass support for this idea. But it was vetoed by the military and, like many drafts, the committee's ended up exactly where it started, with Sykes's idea of a partition that would give Britain control of territory from the Red Sea to the Persian Gulf.

The first inkling the French gained of Sykes's scheme was from the man himself, when he disclosed his thinking to French officials as he passed through Cairo that summer. Alarmed by Sykes's suggestion that the British claim could stretch as far north as Damascus, they reported what he had said to Paris.

In the French capital an imperialist pressure group, the Comité de l'Asie Française, had for several months been pushing their government to lay claim to Syria and Palestine, but their emotional argument that France should reclaim lands she had conquered during the Crusades gained little traction. The rather more concrete news of British scheming from Cairo was a godsend. It forced the French government to take up the matter with London.

One member of the Comité was a former lawyer named François Georges-Picot, who had switched careers to join his country's diplomatic service. Compared to Sykes, Georges-Picot remains an enigmatic figure. But one biographical detail is extremely significant: the year that he decided to make the switch from law to diplomacy was 1898 – the year of Fashoda. France's capitulation to British pressure at Fashoda would have dominated his early years as a diplomat and it is certain that, even seventeen years later, the episode rankled with him because he referred to it repeatedly. Fearing that his country would capitulate again, when news of Sykes's plans reached Paris, he arranged for himself to be posted to London to negotiate a deal on the future of the Middle East. Having served as France's consul in Beirut immediately before the war, he was familiar with the region. He was also determined to defend France's interests very forcefully.

One further revelation – the discovery that Britain was secretly in talks with Sharif Hussein of Mecca – convinced the French that their suspicions of their ally's ambitions in the Middle East were justified. While Sykes's committee had been pondering the fate of the region, the British in Cairo had simultaneously been corresponding in secret with the cantankerous and autocratic ruler of the Islamic holy city of Mecca. Hussein had promised he could swing Middle Eastern Arabia against the Sultan's jihad, if the British helped him break free from Ottoman control.

The British high commissioner in Cairo, Sir Henry McMahon, was responsible for this highly sensitive correspondence and initially dismissed the Sharif's claims as grandiose. But as the Gallipoli campaign turned into a disaster, the appeal of the Sharif's offer grew stronger and McMahon's negotiating position weaker. At the same time he received convincing (but, it transpired, exaggerated) intelligence suggesting that the Sharif was as influential as he claimed to be and just as capable of backing the jihad, if Britain's response was unsatisfactory. Hurriedly McMahon offered his government's support for a large independent Arab state which, because he was aware of Sykes's conflicting intentions, he tried to avoid defining too precisely.

The French ambassador in Cairo only got wind of Sharif Hussein's demand four days later, which he reported to London. With impeccable French logic, he and his government assumed that McMahon would reject the Sharif's demand because it so clearly conflicted with the scheme that Sykes had outlined to them that summer, rather than coming up with a fudge, as McMahon had done.

Ahead of their first meeting with Georges-Picot the British realised that they would now need to admit what they had actually offered to the Sharif. According to one witness at the meeting on 23 November 1915, Georges-Picot reacted to the news with 'complete incredulity'. Syria was 'near the heart of the French,' he told his counterparts, before he deftly linked his refusal to give any ground to the most explosive issue, Britain's failure to pull her weight so far in the war. 'Now, after the expenditure of so many lives, France would never consent to offer independence to the Arabs, though at the beginning of the war she might have done so.'

It was in the aftermath of this disastrous encounter that Sykes attended Downing Street. The vivid minutes of the Cabinet meeting on 16 December record him arguing for 'a belt of English-controlled country' stretching from the coast of Palestine to the head of the Persian Gulf that would not only improve imperial security but prevent the French interfering directly in the politics of Mecca. When Arthur Balfour pressed him about where this cordon's northern frontier with the French zone should lie, Sykes must have gestured to the map. For the minutes of the meeting record him replying, 'I should like to draw a line from the "e" of Acre to the last "k" in Kirkuk.'

When a second meeting with Georges-Picot five days after the Cabinet meeting again ended in an impasse over the ownership of Mosul, the British government turned to Sykes. 'He is certainly a very capable fellow, with plenty of ideas, but at the same time painstaking and careful,' wrote one minister, who was convinced that Sykes was fluent in both Arabic and Turkish when in fact he could speak neither.

Sykes met Georges-Picot for the first time the same afternoon, 21 December, and rapidly hammered out a deal using the Acre–Kirkuk line that he had described to the Cabinet the previous week. Territory to the north of this line, including Mosul, would come under French protection; territory to the south, under the British.

To square the contradictory promise to the Sharif with Georges-Picot's territorial demands and his own idea of a defensive cordon across Arabia, Sykes proposed that each power could exercise full control in specific 'Red' British and 'Blue' French coastal zones within these territories if they wished to. The

misleading implication was that in the desert hinterland between these coloured zones, the Arabs would
enjoy relative independence. But landlocked countries
are usually dependent on their coastal neighbours, and
the evidence suggests that Sykes was perfectly aware
that it was impossible to reconcile the allies' and the
Arab claims. He admitted at one stage that his task
was 'to get [the] Arabs to concede as much as possible
to [the] French and to get our Haifa outlet and Palestine included in our sphere of enterprise in the form of
a French concession to us'.[4]

But Georges-Picot would not concede over Palestine. Sykes wanted it to complete his scheme of imperial defence; Georges-Picot for its prestige. They
reluctantly agreed that the Holy Land should have
an international administration, a compromise that
enabled them to finalise the 'Anglo-French Agreement' on 3 January 1916.

The secret deal was formalised in an exchange of
letters between Britain's and France's foreign minis-
ters that May. Today, the map their two negotiators
signed can be found in Britain's National Archives.
The dividing line, territories and zones are all marked
in coloured pencil. The most intriguing detail is the
signatures, near Basra in the bottom right-hand corner.
Georges-Picot signed in black ink; Sykes, by contrast,
preferred pencil.

Whether conscious or not, the contrasting choice
of writing implements certainly reflected each side's
attitude towards the pact. Georges-Picot, and the

French government more generally, were happy with what he had wrung out of the British and determined to hold them to it; Sykes and his colleagues, on the other hand, were uneasy about the deal, which they convinced themselves was a hypothetical expedient required to reassure the French rather than – as it turned out to be – an oddly resilient blueprint that heavily influenced the post-war negotiations on the future of the region.

The British immediately looked for a way to wriggle out of what they quickly renamed the Sykes–Picot Agreement, starting with the most serious loophole: its unsatisfactory settlement of Palestine. Sooner or later the agreement would become public, and when it did so it would be vulnerable because public hostility to imperialism was growing. Within weeks of signing his name upon the map, Sykes himself had started making overtures to the Zionists. His intention was that Britain should assume sponsorship of their so far unsuccessful campaign to establish a Jewish state in Palestine – a strategy duly publicised in the Balfour Declaration. British imperialism would advance, in Zionist clothing.

Days after the 1918 armistice the British prime minister, Lloyd George, used a meeting with his French counterpart, Georges Clemenceau, to confirm French acquiescence to Britain's claim to Palestine. At the same time he seized on Clemenceau's weakness to demand Mosul (which Sykes had happily conceded to Georges-Picot) because, by then, the importance of its nearby oilfields had dawned on British strategists. Clemenceau needed Lloyd George's support at the impending peace conference in order to regain Alsace-Lorraine and was forced to agree. The eastern end of Sykes's Acre–Kirkuk line was thus rerouted northwards round Mosul, although the border was not finalised until late in the 1920s after Britain had accepted French and American participation in Iraq's (British-dominated) oil company, by which time Sykes was long dead. Military weakness also meant that France was unable to hold the large area of Anatolia it claimed under the agreement against well-organised and motivated Turkish forces led by Mustafa Kemal.

Yet to those who argue that these significant changes destroy the argument that Sykes–Picot had any impact on the region, the awkward fact remains that the deal foresaw the partition of the region between Britain and France, which was what then came to pass once the United States had retreated into isolationism. The need to attract investment to finance oil extraction in Iraq provided a further argument to deny autonomy to the Arabs, who had no recent record of self-government. And finally the likelihood of another global war made Britain unwilling to upset the French. Arthur Balfour put it candidly during the Paris peace negotiations. Although 'we had not been honest with the Arabs or the French,' he admitted, 'it was now preferable to quarrel with the Arabs rather than the French, if there was to be a quarrel at all'.[5]

In 1920 the League of Nations awarded mandates to

France to govern Syria and to Britain for Palestine and Iraq, tasking them with preparing these new countries for rapid independence. In an effort to disrupt rising Arab fury at this outcome, both mandated powers then subdivided their new possessions. The French carved Lebanon from Syria in an attempt to create a predominantly Christian bridgehead. The British, facing uproar in Palestine for their support for Jewish immigration, divided the mandate in two down the rift valley, creating Transjordan. To make amends, and further confuse opponents, they parachuted in two of the Sharif's sons to rule Jordan and Iraq. The French embarked on a cynical policy of divide and rule that explains, for instance, why the Alawite sect, to which Bashar al-Assad belongs, still dominates the Syrian army and society.

Soon after the League of Nations had awarded the mandates, it made the mandatory powers responsible for defining their borders. The dividing line that Sykes suggested to the Cabinet five years earlier inspired an interim frontier between Lebanon and Palestine, and between Syria and Jordan and Iraq as far as the Euphrates. It was refined and eventually finalised, once the greater question of the status of Mosul had been resolved, in 1931. Local politics and rivalry between British and French political officers failed to change it substantially from the crayon line that Sykes and Georges-Picot had drawn on their map. Sykes's idea of 'a belt of English-controlled country' survives today in the way that Jordan joins the two other countries once run by Britain, Israel and Iraq, keeping Syria and Saudi Arabia apart.

Oddly, however, it was less what the Sykes-Picot Agreement did and more what it didn't do that makes it resonate. Given Britain's promise to the Sharif, its failure to acknowledge Arab aspirations provided evidence of bad faith. Its failure to resolve the future of Palestine led the British, with terrible consequences, to pursue an alliance with the Zionists that precipitated the Arab-Israeli conflict.

One is left wondering what might have happened had the British committee's tantalising alternative of semi-autonomy for the Ottoman provinces prevailed. Certainly, it would have given these provinces no more than a semblance of self-rule in the short run. But, in the era of mounting scepticism about empire and amid the calls for self-determination that followed, it might have provided a better basis for transition. However, the exigencies of war and fears for the Entente were not conducive to risk-taking. Instead a settlement that was anachronistic from the outset was imposed. The primacy of great power politics over local aspirations ensured that the Sykes–Picot Agreement was a crucial influence on the political geography and recent history of the Middle East.

# WHY DID YOU RENAME YOUR SON? DIARIES OF THE GREAT WAR FROM THE OTTOMAN FRONT

## Salim Tamari

THE GREAT WAR on the Eastern Front, reconsidered after the passage of a century, led to major transformations in the way in which the people of the region – from the Ottoman capital of Istanbul to the Arab provinces of the empire – looked at themselves and at the world. What I propose to do is to see how the war and the fighting were reflected in the biographical trajectories of soldiers who fought in it and civilians who endured it, and how the war affected the transformation of their lives and the reshaping of their identity and affiliations during and after the war.

The First World War was fought in the east on four Ottoman fronts. One was the Caucasian front with the Russians; the second was in southern Iraq, mainly around Basra and Kut al Amar; the third, at Suez, Sinai and Beersheba, was known as the Palestine front. The principal front, as far as the Ottoman leadership was concerned, was fought in the Dardanelles at Gallipoli, or Çanakkale as it is known in Turkish, where the main encounter with the British and the Anzac forces took place under the command of Mustapha Kemal, later known as Atatürk and the founder of the Turkish Republic.

The war was so devastating that, according to contemporary accounts, it destroyed one-sixth of the total population of Greater Syria – one of the highest death tolls on all war fronts during that period. The victims, both civilians and combatants, perished as a result of the fighting, hunger, famine and diseases. Tens of thousands of civilians died because of the British naval blockade on food supplies coming into ports like Jaffa and Beirut, as well as from Ottoman governor Jamal Pasha's sequestration of crops for the Fourth and Fifth Army Corps in Syria. The urban landscape was devastated in a way that recalls, under different circumstances, the destruction that we witness today in Syria and Iraq. At the time, Greater Syria – that is, the Ottoman provinces of Bilad al-Sham, which included Palestine and Mount Lebanon – suffered the highest proportion of deaths of any region in the world, even when compared with Belgium, Britain, Germany and France. The scale of the devastation, although for a smaller population, had a much greater impact in terms of the denuding of the countryside, the dislocation of the urban centres and the disappearance of the younger male population.

: :

The first three memoirs I will examine were written by civilians, among a number of texts published by literary figures from the Arab provinces of the Ottoman Empire. Those narratives were published in the form of diaries and memoirs, as well as in semi-fictional accounts. The writers include Khalil Sakakini, who kept a daily diary during the war in Jerusalem. His account is riveting in that it conveys a vivid portrait of the desolation of the city in 1915 and 1916, the famine years. One of Sakakini's most moving episodes concerns the so-called Volunteer Labour Brigades (*tawabeer al 'amaleh*), which mobilised older residents of the region on the home front to perform menial tasks such as street cleaning and digging trenches. Towards the end of 1917 Sakakini was arrested for harbouring the Hebrew poet Alter Levine, who was suspected of spying for the allies. Sakakini was chained and tied to Levine and force-marched to Damascus, where he spent the final days of the war in prison. He later escaped and joined the forces of Emir Faisal in Jabal Druze, then engaged in the Arab Revolt against the Ottomans, where he wrote the anthem of the first, short-lived independent Arab state.

Muhammad Kurd Ali's Damascene memoirs cover his period as a publicist – some critics would say apologist – for the excesses of Jamal and Anwar (Enver) Pashas in Syria and Palestine. He was the chief organiser of two expeditions of Arab public figures and intellectuals to Gallipoli and Medina (in the Arabian Peninsula) to defend the war effort and bring the experiences of the fighters to the general Arab public. He was also active in the advocacy of Arab–Turkish bilingualism in the Ottoman administration, including the schooling and court system, as a means of integrating the Arabs into the Ottoman system. During the war he became editor of the newspaper *al-Sharq*, Jamal Pasha's instrument for propaganda in the Arab provinces. Today Kurd Ali is best known as the author of the *Khitat ash-Sham* (*Chronicles of Syria*), a multivolume work covering the geography and history of Greater Syria over six centuries, and a treatise of Ottoman modernity in the Levant. His war memoirs, however, were remembered as a blot on his integrity as a scholar and he was criticised as an apologist for Ottoman attacks on 'Arab separatism' – that is, on his fellow countrymen who were allied with the Arab nationalists against the Ottomans.

The most important fictional work to come out of the Great War in Arabic is *The Life of Mifleh al-Ghassani* (1921) by the Palestinian writer and journalist Najib Nassar. Subtitled 'A Page from the Events of the Great War', the novella is a thinly disguised autobiographical war memoir of the author, who spent 1916–17 hiding from the Turkish gendarmes in the Bedouin encampments of the Jordan Valley, escaping possible execution on charges of being pro-British. Nassar also published the combative *al-Karmil* newspaper in Haifa, a satirical newspaper that became known for its defence of peasants' rights and attacks on Zionist land purchases. He published *The Life of*

*Mifleh al-Ghassani* in serial form in *al-Karmil* and later as a book in the early days of the Mandate. Almost half of the book deals with his capture, interrogation, trial and eventual release from imprisonment in Damascus.

Nassar successfully defended himself against all charges and was acquitted by the Martial Court of Damascus. The fictional format allowed him to construct extensive dialogues with imaginary and real companions, soldiers, officers, prisoners, Bedouins and with his ultimate nemesis, Jamal Pasha, who nonetheless sincerely believed in his innocence and pressed for his release behind the scenes. All the events and characters in the story were built on real people and events that can be corroborated from external sources.

Mifleh/Nassar's account of his trial in the military tribunal contains a farcical moment that identifies a second list of charges. In the first list he is accused of hostility to the ruling party in Istanbul, the Committee of Union and Progress (CUP), to the government, nominally headed by the Sultan but controlled by the 'Three Pashas' and in particular Enver Pasha, and to the German army. He is also accused of being pro-British and favouring Arab separatism. In a second meeting of the court he is questioned about changing the name of his son from Anwar (Enver) to Adib. Here is the exchange in my translation:

MILITARY JUDGE: Following the Constitutional Revolution [1908] you named your newborn son

Anwar, after the unionist leader and war minister Enver Pasha, then it seems you changed his name.

MIFLEH: Yes, it is true I named my second son Anwar, in celebration of the hero of the constitution. I changed his name to Adib later not because I lost faith in the unionists, but because Anwar Bey deserted the Arabs in Tripoli [Libya, where the Ottoman army, alongside Arab tribesmen, fought Italy from October 1911 to November 1912] and left them to fight the Italians without leadership.

MILITARY JUDGE: What was Enver Pasha to do at the time, when the Ottoman government concluded a peace agreement with the Italians and ordered him to withdraw his troops?

MIFLEH: In my modest view he should have resigned from his commission and continued to fight the Italians to the end, instead of allowing this Arab province to be removed from the body of the Ottoman sultanate, and undermining the loyalty of the Arabs to the state.

When asked about his partisan views, Mifleh declares that he was never an enemy of the unionists, but he was against their Turkification schemes, which weakened the bonds of loyalty of the Arabs towards the state. To the charge of being pro-British, Mifleh did not hide his Anglophilia and answered that he had favoured an alliance with the British over an alliance with Germany before the war, but once war was declared, 'Then – I wrote in the daily press – we have to talk in the tongue of the government, see with its eyes, and hear with its ears.'[1]

The vindication of Nassar's stance in his real trial, as well as in the fictional trial of Mifleh al-Ghassani, is used in the novel to illustrate both the protagonist's commitment to the principle of non-intervention in the war and his loyalty to the Ottoman Empire, despite his relentless criticism of the Turkification scheme of the CUP government. But the novel also demonstrates a degree of integrity in the military court system, since he successfully overturned the charge sheet accusing him of desertion and betrayal.

⋮ ⋮

The second set of diaries and memoirs examined here contains soldiers' writings. Such narratives of the war were rarer, in large part because literacy was limited, but also because the diaries tended not to survive the consequences of exile, trench warfare and fear of discovery. Here I will examine the narratives in three soldiers' diaries that reached us against the odds. They allow us to examine how events affected the lives of three Ottoman (Arab and Turkish) soldiers. Their narratives are doubly significant because, contrary to popular assumptions, the manner in which the war affected their consciousness did not always correspond to their ethnic background.

The first was a soldier known as Mehmet Fesih

(Muhammad al Fasih), who came from a mixed Turkish–Arab family in Mersin, a frontier area in the Turkish–Arab divide of the Ottoman sultanate. He fought in Gaza and in Gallipoli where he kept a daily diary of his observations. *Mulazim* (Lieutenant) Fesih occupied a liminal position in the nascent ethnic divide that separated southern Anatolia from northern Syria. Belonging to a family that combined Arabic and Turkish as their spoken language, he would nevertheless choose to identify with and fight for the Kemalist forces. While his diary is replete with references to the communal solidarity of the various ethnic groups that made up the Ottoman army, particularly to his Syrian comrades at Gallipoli/Çanakkale, he would make his decision in favour of the post-war Republican movement and the new Turkish nationalism it embodied. After the termination of the Great War, he volunteered to fight against the invading European and Greek forces, where his contribution was duly recognised and rewarded. He eventually Turkified his name, in adherence to the diktat of Kemalist ideology, and became a general in the Republican army.

The second narrative is that of Second Lieutenant Aref Shehadeh, a junior officer in the Fifth Army Corps, who was from a Jerusalem family of merchants. In April 1915 he was captured by the tsarist army in fighting at Erzurum on the Caucasian front and spent the bulk of the war years in an internment camp for German and Ottoman prisoners in Krasnoyarsk, Siberia. In the Siberian camp, in common with many soldiers who were captured in the war, he began to reflect on his destiny. He records how the Siberian exile made him reflect on his national identity in a manner he was not aware of until he later joined one of the literary clubs in Istanbul:

> I was not aware that I was an Arab, and that I
> should think of the future of my Arab nation
> until the establishment of the Literary Forum (al
> Muntada al Adabi) in Istanbul. Of the founders
> I remember four names: Abdul Karim al Khalil,
> Yusif Mukhaibar, Jamil al Husseini, and Seiful
> Din al Khatib. I was registered as a member and
> was since then engulfed with the prevailing Arab
> nationalism among the students. It was then
> that I began to hear the words Arabs, Arabism,
> Nationalism, and Homeland (Krasnoyarsk,
> Siberia, 8 February 1917).[2]

During the first two years of internment he lived in common quarters with Turkish officers, lectured and wrote in Turkish, and was generally loyal to the Ottoman war aims. The Hijazi revolt of Sharif Hussein and the Syrian nationalists in Damascus for Arab independence from the Ottoman Empire, known as the Arab Revolt, compelled him to rethink his Ottoman loyalties in favour of an amorphous Arabness. In this regard the Russian command played a significant role in encouraging Arab separatism by keeping the living quarters of Arab and Turkish officers apart, and

*Lt. Aref Shehadeh's Prison Camp Identity Card, Krosnayersk, Siberia, 1915 (Institute of Palestine Studies Archives)*

extending favouritism to Syrian detainees in terms of passes to leave the camp and access to newspapers and the outside world. In this process Shehadeh shifted his loyalties from adherence to the principles of Osmenlilik (Ottomanist constitutional ideology) to those of Arab independence.

We should keep in mind, though, that these claims of a sudden awakening, however sincere, were made retrospectively by Shehadeh in the shadow of Ottoman military defeat and his escape from Siberia to join the forces of Prince Faisal in southern Syria. After the war Shehadeh became editor of *Suriyyah al-Janubiyyah*, an organ of the Faisali movement in Palestine. He adopted the name of Aref al-Aref and became a prominent historian of Jerusalem, but his writings continued to reflect his early Ottomanism in Istanbul and in his Siberian exile.

This issue of national dualism, ethnic ambivalence and reinvention of identity is exemplified differently, through the prism of pacifism in war, in the experiences of the third soldier in this trilogy. Ihsan Turjman, a clerk in the Ottoman Fourth Army, was stationed in Jerusalem. He fought briefly on the Suez front and perished towards the end of the war, in 1917. His situation was exceptional because he was a self-proclaimed pacifist. He hated the war and he was desperate for it to end. He recorded in his diary in excruciating detail the degradation experienced by the inhabitants of Jerusalem and Palestine during the locust attack and famine of 1915. In December 1915, he wrote: 'I haven't seen darker days in my life. Flour and bread have basically disappeared since last Saturday … We have so far tolerated living without rice, sugar and kerosene. But how can we live without bread?' He also dwells on the extreme measures taken by his compatriots in order to survive, including prostitution and desertion.

*A page from the diary of Private Ihsan al Turjman, Jerusalem,*
*30 March, 1915 (Turjman Family Papers, by permission)*

Diary writing was rare but not altogether uncommon among soldiers on the Ottoman front. Those who were literate were aware of the need to record their impressions of the war for posterity. This is how Turjman opens his second diary:

Jerusalem, Sunday the 28th of March [Gregorian], 1915, Mart 1331 [Ottoman Fiscal Calendar]

Two years ago I began to keep a daily diary. But I soon neglected the routine and started writing occasionally until I quit writing altogether.

This evening I went to visit Khalil Effendi al Sakakini, in the company of Hasan Khalidi and

Omar al Salih. Khalil Effendi read to us from his diary. It so excited me that I decided to re-start my own memoirs. Our conversation revolved around this miserable war, and how long it is likely to continue, and about the fate of this [Ottoman] state. We more or less agreed that the days of the state were numbered, and that its dismemberment was imminent.

But what will be the fate of Palestine? We all saw two possibilities: independence or annexation to Egypt. The last possibility is more likely since only the English are likely to possess this country, and England is unlikely to give full sovereignty to Palestine, but is more liable to annex it to Egypt, and create a single dominion ruled by the Khedive of Egypt. Egypt is our neighbour and since both countries contain a majority of Muslims, it makes sense to annex it and crown the Viceroy of Egypt as King of Palestine and Hijaz. Rumours abound in the street today. We heard that the English fleet has bombarded Haifa, and that several English frigates crossed the Dardanelles until they reached the Sea of Marmara. Even if this item is not true, it will soon be realized since the Dardanelles have been hammered relentlessly [by Allied ships] and cannot resist the British fleet forever. The city of [...] fell today in Austria. This is most likely to change the course of the war, and bring our deliverance nearer.[3]

This entry is also exceptional in that it reveals political debates that were being discussed by soldiers and officers on the front, and in army administrative headquarters, where Turjman was employed. He raises, for example, questions about expectations for the future of Palestine after the war. Three options are suggested. One was for Palestine to become part of Syria and separate from the Ottomans. The second was to remain an Ottoman province through the struggle for autonomy under the aegis of common Ottoman citizenship. But Turjman talks also about a third alternative, which today may sound extraordinary. Namely, that the future of Palestine lies in unity with Khedival Egypt. That was apparently an opinion that many people thought was natural because the Egyptian links, through trade and commerce, as well as cultural exchanges (newspapers, music and theatrical troupes), were common and frequent, even during the war period. The future of Palestine and Syria being with Egypt was therefore seen as a possibility, on an equal footing with independent Syria and autonomy within the empire. In his diary Turjman makes numerous references to the 'degenerate' lifestyle of the Ottoman military leadership, and their lack of credibility. He was proud of the Sharifian rebellion in the Hijaz and full of criticism of the 'servility' of the 'Syrian and Palestinian people' who failed to rise up and fight for their freedom. He also makes oblique references to the Zionists in the context of Jamal Pasha's presumed Jewish mistress, Lea Tannenbaum, but his thoughts on the Zionist political project were unrecorded.

In Gallipoli, the battle which became an icon for Ottoman resilience in defence of the Fatherland, one forgets that more than half the war dead came from non-Turkish regions of the empire – they were Bulgarians, Albanians, Kurds, Arabs and Armenians. Of the two battalions that fought with Mustafa Kemal in Gallipoli, the majority of combatants, as well as the dead, were reportedly Syrian Arab soldiers. Yet those indicators of Ottoman solidarity were soon replaced by Turkish nationalist iconography, and the story was retold retrospectively as a Turkish victory against the invading allies. The Ottoman victims were now rebaptised, post-mortem, as Turkish martyrs. In this conspiracy of silence, Arab and Turkish historiography colluded in excluding the nature of the multi-ethnic character of the sultanate, and of the officers and soldiers who fought under its banner. European historiography, similarly, became preoccupied with the tragic use of Anzac soldiers as cannon fodder by the British Empire. To them the significance of Gallipoli was its singularity in giving birth to Australian nationhood.

⋮ ⋮

The biographic trajectories of the three soldiers suggest several responses by soldiers to their experience of war: rethinking and reinvention of identity (Fesih); separatist nationalism (Shehadeh); and pacifism (Turjman). I draw two conclusions from this discussion. First, the reconstruction of identity experienced

in the Great War was fluid. Self-conceptions transform themselves through ruptures very quickly during
times of war, because war disrupts the tempo of daily
routine. It compels us to rethink where we are and
where we are heading in the immediate future. The
second conclusion is that, when people are faced with
devastation, they tend to revert to the comfort and
security of local identity, because it is protective and
familiar and allows people to insulate themselves from
what seems to be the impending collapse of the world
around them. Such reversions are apparent in the war
and devastation that are happening today.

However, unlike the 'localism' of today's Syria and
Iraq, which have reverted to homologous religious
sectarianism, the protectionist localism of the Great
War was communal, and existed peacefully with the
rising secular nationalism of Damascus, Beirut and
Istanbul. But if ordinary soldiers sought a protective reversion to the comforts of localism, the civilians discussed here reacted to the devastation in the
opposite direction. Sakakini sought an assertion of a
common humanist bond, that transcended nationalism (Arab and Turkish), Muhammad Kurd Ali
became an advocate of Greater Syrian unity, while
Najib Nassar, the doyen of Palestinian journalists – as
he later became known – took to a class perspective,
defending peasants' land rights and tribal entitlement, in honour of the nameless people who hid and
defended him when he was pursued by the authorities.

The ideological choices made by these three

soldiers and three civilians were often the result of contingencies of geography and lineage: that is, they were dictated mostly by where they lived, where they grew up and how they thought of their family origins. But the ultimate determining factor in their choices was the devastating war which led to the death of the Ottoman idea – the conceptual framework that had been able to mobilise hundreds of thousands of imperial subjects to fight for the Sultan, an array of committed intellectuals behind them, under the rubric of common citizenship and a multi-ethnic homeland.

# IN THE PRESENT TENSE

## The Unravelling of the Old Order

# OPENING POLITICS' BLACK BOX: REFLECTIONS ON THE PAST, PRESENT AND FUTURE OF THE EGYPTIAN REVOLUTION

## Khaled Fahmy

ON 25 JANUARY 2011, I went to *midan Tahrir* (Liberation Square) to join what I thought would be yet another small demonstration doomed to be crushed by overwhelming police force. The minute I stepped into the square, however, I realised that this time the situation was different. For one thing, our numbers were huge. For another, the slogans were new. There was the same beat as familiar slogans, but now I heard strange, unrecognisable words. Soon, I figured out what people were shouting: '*Al-sha'b.*' Stop. '*Yurid.*' Stop. '*Isqat al-Nizam.*' Stop. 'The people.' 'Demand.' 'The downfall of the regime.' Goosebumps spread all over my body. I then found myself joining tens of thousands of fellow citizens at the top of my voice.

For the following eighteen days, I went to Tahrir nearly every day, returning home only to sleep and to get provisions for my friends who preferred to camp in the square. Mubarak's step-down was only a matter of time, we firmly believed. The regime is teetering on the brink of collapse. We are finally making our voice heard. We are shaping our country's future. And soon a new slogan spread like wildfire throughout the huge *midan* and was repeated by hundreds of thousands of people from all walks of life: 'Irfa' rasak fo'. Inta Masri.' 'Lift up your head. You're Egyptian.'

Four years later, this confident, hopeful mood is no more. Instead of the open, democratic country that seemed, for a short while, to be ours at last, Egypt is now in the grip of a military dictatorship that has arrested our friends, imprisoned our comrades and quashed our dreams. Kangaroo trials have passed death sentences on hundreds of Islamists in sessions that lasted less than an hour. And on 14 August 2013 security forces committed what Human Rights Watch described as one of the world's largest killings of demonstrators on a single day in recent history, a massacre in Raba'a Square in Cairo that was more lethal than what took place in Tiananmen Square and that probably amounts to a crime against humanity.

How did the eighteen days in Tahrir that saw so many Egyptians embrace these lofty ideals lead to twelve hours in Raba'a Square that witnessed a massacre in which more than 800 people were killed? How did we start in such a hope-filled way in 2011 and end up with this bloody massacre in 2013? How did the Arab Spring morph into an Arab nightmare, out of which we seem not to be able to awaken?

⫶ ⫶

I am a historian by training, so I will offer a historical reading of the Arab Spring – particularly in Egypt, but applicable to some extent, I think, to other countries involved in the Arab Spring. Thus I will not only reflect on the events of only the past four years, but will consider the revolution's deeper historical roots.

One way to do so is by reflecting on a peculiar personal experience. Only a week after Mubarak stepped down, the head of the Egyptian National Archives, together with the Minister of Culture, appointed me as chair of an official committee whose mandate was to document the momentous events the country had just witnessed. I assembled a team of archivists, historians and IT experts, and we set about laying down criteria for accomplishing the mammoth task ahead of us.

We soon found ourselves having to answer some difficult questions: 'How do we go about collecting people's testimonies?' and, even more problematic, 'Given that we are effectively a government committee, can we guarantee that the testimonies do not end up falling into the hands of security agencies and are not used against the very people who entrusted us with these potentially self-incriminating testimonies?'

However, there were even more difficult questions to deal with. Some of these were historical. When did the revolution end? Did it end with Mubarak's step-down? With the constitutional amendments? With the parliamentary elections? With the presidential elections? And given that we are constantly attending funerals of friends and loved ones, running from one police station to another looking for friends who have been arrested, and participating in demonstrations and sit-ins to demand the release of our comrades – given all this, did the revolution actually end, or is it still going on?

Most difficult of all were questions not about when and how the revolution ended, if it ever did, but when it began and where it originated. Was it launched on 25 January, National Police Day, when we took to the streets to protest against the endemic use of torture in prisons and other places of detention? Or did it begin on 14 January, when Ben Ali, the Tunisian president fled his country to Saudi Arabia, inspiring people in Egypt to say, 'If the Tunisians can do it, then maybe we can too.' Or was its beginning on New Year's Eve 2010, when Muslims and Copts took to the streets to protest against what they believed was their government's complicity in the bombing of churches? Or a few months earlier, with the beating to death of the young Alexandrian activist Khaled Said, who later became the icon of the revolution? Did it start in 2008, when thousands took to the streets all over the country in solidarity with the striking workers in the industrial town of Mahalla? Or were its origins in 2004 with the birth of the Kefaya [Enough] Movement, whose members were protesting, week in and week out, against Mubarak's dictatorial rule? Did it start in March 2003, when we took to the streets protesting against the US bombing of Iraq and when we occupied Tahrir for a few hours? Or did it begin in March 2000, when the Israeli prime minister paid his ill-fated visit to al-Haram al-Sharif in Jerusalem, prompting thousands of Egyptian university students to spill out of their university gates and to demonstrate in solidarity with the Second Palestinian Intifada?

My colleagues on the committee and I pondered these questions, and even more difficult ones. During the last of his long years in office, were we demonstrating against Mubarak for grooming his son to take over the presidency and effectively transform the republic into a monarchy? Were we demonstrating against the endemic use of torture by the Egyptian police? Were we demonstrating against the debased choice that Mubarak presented us with whereby he was effectively telling us, 'Either accept my torture chambers or Islamist rule'?

Or did our revolution have deeper roots still? Was it in fact a revolution not only against Mubarak's thirty black years, but against the July Regime set down sixty years earlier in the wake of the 25 July 1952 revolution? That revolution offered us another debased choice: giving up our constitutional and political rights in exchange for social and economic rights. Were we rebelling to assert our entitlement to have both kinds of rights: constitutional and political, as well as social and economic? When we took to the streets on 25 January 2011, and when we finally overwhelmed the police by our numbers, determination and tenacity on 28 January, the Friday of Rage, were we doing what we, as Egyptian people, should have done in the wake of the catastrophic defeat of 6 June 1967, when, instead of asking then President Gamal Abdul Nasser to step down and face trial, we actually begged him to rescind his resignation and stay on as uncontested leader of the nation?

Or was it possible that our revolution had even deeper roots? Were we protesting against the very nature of the modern Egyptian state, a state that was put in place by Mehmed Ali in 1805? When this Macedonian adventurer set about changing the status of Egypt from a mere province of the Ottoman Empire to a special realm that he and his sons could rule for a hundred years, he founded an army that would dominate all aspects of Egyptian life and change the nature of the country for ever. Were we specifically rebelling against the state that was created as a result of establishing this army, an army which enslaved peasants by dragging them against their wishes to serve dynastic interests that made no sense to them, to struggle for a cause in which they did not believe and to die in wars that were not theirs?

⋮ ⋮

These are the questions that I found myself pondering when I set about chairing the committee that was to document the 25 January revolution. And they made me see that we Egyptians were revolting not only against Mubarak and his cronies, but against this state which, to paraphrase Marx, came dripping from head to foot, from every pore, with dirt and blood. The modern Egyptian state was not founded on the flimsiest notion of constitutionalism or the rule of law. We entered into no social contract that tied us to our ruler, who descended upon us with his cronies like vultures ravaging town and country. This is a state that has repeatedly failed its citizens, is inherently despotic and is suffering from a foundational legitimacy crisis.

For the past two hundred years, we have not spared any effort in rebelling against this tyrannical state. In contrast to what we are told in our schools, we did not revolt only against foreign invaders, be they French or British. We also resisted this domestic leviathan by every means at our disposal.

In 1821, and in the wake of higher taxation, more frequent corvée (forced labour) levies, a draconian monopolies policy and, above all, an unprecedented conscription policy, Egyptian peasants revolted in a massive popular uprising in the south, which spread from Qina to Aswan and in which 20,000 men and women participated, resulting in the death of 3,000 peasants. The following year, an equally large uprising spread in the Delta and was quelled by six machine guns commanded by Mehmed Ali in person. In 1844 another large uprising erupted in Menoufiya in the Delta, where government warehouses were set on fire and the pasha's agents taken hostage. There were also cases where peasants were reported to have uprooted the cotton plants from their fields, despite the fact that, cotton being a lucrative cash crop, this extreme act would have cost them dearly. In 1863 a large uprising again erupted in the south, in the same area as the uprising forty years earlier.

In 1879–82 Egyptians from a wide range of social, economic and political backgrounds rose up in a nationwide revolution under Ahmed Urabi with the aim of subjecting this leviathan state to constitutional rule, defining the rights and responsibilities of the Khedive, the monarchial ruler, separating his purse from the public purse and putting limits on his power. The revolution was on the cusp of succeeding, before it was aborted by blatant European intervention. On 11 July 1882 the British navy, answering the Khedive's call for help in confronting this constitutional movement, bombarded Alexandria and succeeded in defeating Urabi's troops, thereby inaugurating a military occupation that would last seventy-odd years.

The British occupation dissipated our revolutionary energies and we now found ourselves having to fight for constitutional rights and for independence at the same time. Three and a half decades after the defeat of Urabi's army and the landing on Egyptian soil of British troops, we rose in one massive revolution in 1919, asking for both independence and a constitution. However, the much-anticipated liberation from occupation fell far short of the revolution's expectations, for in 1922 the British handed Egypt a truncated independence that allowed British troops to stay on Egyptian soil and deprived Egypt of the right to shape its own foreign policy. More seriously, the British inter-fered in the constitution-writing process, with the result that the 1923 Constitution was tilted towards the palace and gave the crown significant powers that enabled it to dominate parliament.

The so-called golden age of Egypt's liberalism, 1923–52, was neither golden nor liberal. With the British maintaining their grip over our country, with a king using constitutional licence to dissolve parlia-ment at will and with political parties failing to develop strategies to defeat either the colonial occupier or local tyranny, the moment was ripe for us to take to the streets and for mass politics to surface.

This political stalemate was eventually broken in 1952, when Gamal Abdul Nasser and his junta staged a coup that abolished the monarchy, suspended parliamentary politics, persecuted all major political players of the ancien régime, rounded up thousands of communists and sent them to remote prisons, and arrested tens of thousands of Muslim Brotherhood members and subjected them to horrifying torture. Those of us who were not tortured, imprisoned or exiled found ourselves marching in unison behind our leader straight to a dark abyss. Following the June 1967 War, we rose again and protested against the lenient sentences that those responsible for this cata-strophic defeat had received. A couple of years later, our universities burst at the seams with demonstra-tions against a seemingly indecisive policy towards our erstwhile foreign enemy, Israel. In 1977 we took to the streets again in massive numbers against the government's economic austerity measures. Nine years later, our brethren in the Central Security Forces rose in one massive uprising against the draconian conditions of their conscription. And fourteen years later we took to the streets in large numbers protesting against Israeli Prime Minister Sharon's visit to al-Haram al-Sharif, bringing us back full circle to the immediate causes of the 25 January revolution.

⋮ ⋮

Far from being a Facebook phenomenon, a foreign conspiracy or an insurrection staged by a handful of street urchins, as members of the current regime insist in their phantasmagorical delusions, our revolution has a long and venerable pedigree. We the people have been in a state of constant rebellion for the past two hundred years, and 25 January was but the latest phase of our struggle to force the tyrannical state to serve us, instead of we serving it.

Why has it proved so difficult for us to end our status as subjects in our own country and to force our state to treat us as citizens? Five reasons stood, and still stand, in the way of democracy in Egypt and indeed in the whole of the Arab world.

First, our colonial past and post-colonial present show that, despite their deafening rhetoric, Western powers have not spared any effort to thwart our struggle for democracy. As noted above, the British not only crushed our first constitutional movement in 1881–2, but also made sure to distort our second attempt when they intervened in the writing of the 1923 Constitution to tip the balance in favour of their pliant client king and against the nascent parliament. When Britain's moment in the Middle East came to an end and the United States took over as the global superpower, Washington did not miss an opportunity to support our dictators, just as it did in neighbouring countries.

Second, not only has the century-long Arab–Israeli conflict sapped our energy and diverted precious resources, but our despots have also used it cynically to postpone indefinitely democratic reforms. 'No call to top the call for battle' was a slogan deployed domestically to silence all calls for accountability, transparency and civic participation. Moreover, our struggle with Israel necessitated the expansion of the military, and when this military failed in its mission at the borders, it diverted its energies to the domestic sphere and transformed itself into a mighty economic and political player that rightly saw democracy as inimical to its interests.

Third, the scourge of petro-dollars meant that the oil-rich despotic regimes of the Gulf could interfere in our country and support anti-democratic forces. The success of the counter-revolution following 30 June 2013 could not be understood without factoring in the billions of dollars that both Saudi Arabia and the UAE paid the new Egyptian regime under General Sisi.

Fourth, the tragedy of our current revolution also

lies in our inability to look back to our modern history and choose a moment that we would like to resurrect. We have no 'reset button' that we can press to jump-start our history; no one specific dark moment that we can simply wish away; no isolated anomalous period that we would like to suppress; no imagined golden age in which we can claim we shaped our destiny and to which we want to return.

Fifth, and to make things even more difficult, the tragedy of our country now, and indeed of other Arab Spring countries, is that in attempting to tame this domestic leviathan, we in Egypt, Libya and Syria find that we have opened another Pandora's box, that of political Islam. For we find ourselves asking not only what the role of the army in the state should be but also what role religion should play in politics. This, in turn, has opened up all kinds of deep existential questions that we as Egyptians and Arabs have been struggling with for the past hundred years.

⋮ ⋮

Despite these deep problems, I remain confident that the future is ours and that our revolution will prevail. This may not happen next month, next year or even in the next decade. Given how deep are the roots of and reasons for this revolution, it would be naive to expect its victory overnight with one decisive knockout blow. Nevertheless, and despite the recent gains by the counter-revolution, I am firmly convinced that the future is ours and that we are now witnessing the beginning of the end of this tyrannical state.

My optimism derives from two simple but profound facts. The first is that we the people have asserted our presence in our own country. We have a will; we have a voice; and we have agency. We acted in history and affected a radical change – never before in our long history that extends far back to the pharaohs have we managed to topple a leader from power. In the January revolution we did that, and we thus asserted our right and determination to shape our own destiny.

We have also prised open the black box of politics. Politics is no longer what government officials, security agents or army officers decide among themselves. It is also no longer what university students demonstrate about, what workers in their factories struggle about or young men in mosques whisper about. Politics is now the stuff of gossip in coffee shops, of housewives' chats, of metro conversations, even of pillow talk. People now see the political in the quotidian. The genie is out of the bottle and no amount of repression can force it back in.

# CRACKED CAULDRONS: THE FAILURE OF STATES AND THE RISE OF NEW NARRATIVES IN THE MIDDLE EAST

## Tamim al-Barghouti

IN THE ARAB MIDDLE EAST, colonially created modern nation-states have failed in performing their most basic functions, the Hobbesian imperatives for which humans invented states in the first place, preventing civil war or foreign invasion, let alone fostering economic development, social welfare or human rights. In the past few decades, their resounding failure has led to the emergence of new forms of political organisation, based on sub-state and supra-state identities where narratives are replacing structures, networks are replacing hierarchical pyramids, conviction is replacing obedience, improvisation from the peripheries is replacing central planning, and ideas, for better or for worse, are replacing leaders.

This fading away of the colonially created modern Arab nation-state, and its replacement with ethnic, religious and ideological identities, is a process that can express itself in terms of peaceful democratic uprisings, as in Egypt and Tunisia, or in sectarian or tribal civil wars, as in Libya and Syria. The likelihood of civil war increases if the concerned Arab society is divided along ethnic or sectarian lines and if there are regional and international interests supporting both sides of such divides. Yet these are wars of attrition in which no one party can claim definite victory. Eventually, after civil wars exhaust their parties, the political drive to unite divided societies will enhance the calls to face the historical common enemy, hence recreating a unifying discourse/narrative/identity. Therefore, one can safely argue that, if no peaceful resolution is found to the Arab–Israeli conflict, within the coming two decades a major war between Israel and an array of Middle Eastern entities, state and non-state actors alike, is likely to take place.

Modern Arab states failed on their own terms; they did not reach the benchmarks they set for themselves. Regime after regime, leader after leader, ruling party after ruling party, claimed that they had to sacrifice democracy for economic progress, individual human rights for collective independence, and political change for peace and stability, yet they ended up without stability, peace or independence, instead wallowing in foreign domination, domestic despotism, civil war, poverty, underdevelopment and a painful loss of dignity at all levels of human existence. The image of the mighty military dictator waving to the cheering crowds has become nothing more than a real-life caricature seen by the whole world except by the dictator himself. The dictator's confident sunglasses, his exuberant brass medals and the headgear that expresses his identity crisis as it varies from the traditional keffiyeh to the European hat to the military peaked cap adorned with gold no longer conjure up the intended awe. Instead, they remind the spectators of sixty years of military defeats against Israel, of the hundreds of thousands of infants who died during the American twelve-year-siege and subsequent occupation of Iraq, of the Lebanese, the Syrian, the Algerian, the Sudanese and the Yemeni civil wars, of ragged beggars in the streets of Egypt and the bloodstained walls in Egyptian torture chambers.

This failure of the modern Arab states is structural. It is my argument that the reasons for such failure lie in their colonial origin. It is much less costly for an invading power to control a colonised territory through the collaboration of a group of natives than to control it directly. To perform this duty, this native elite must have two qualities: legitimacy among their own people and the desire to collaborate with the foreign colonial power. So native leaders must be national heroes for their treason to be of any value. If they lacked legitimacy, they would have to rely on sheer force, just like the foreign colonial invaders, thus losing their comparative advantage; if they lacked the will to collaborate, there would be no point in employing them to secure colonial interests. The native elite running the colonially created state thus finds itself in a predicament: it has to acquire domestic legitimacy by opposing the colonial power and has to achieve international recognition by collaborating with that power. To solve this contradiction, the native elite commits itself to securing colonial interests with native hands; the international treaties documenting such commitments then constitute the legal basis for independence. Thus dependence becomes the precondition for independence and servitude the precondition for sovereignty.

This predicament causes the Arab ruling elites to adopt two contradictory discourses: one directed at the domestic audience promising real independence, the liberation of Palestine, Arab and/or Islamic unity, and breaking away from Western domination – in other words changing the status quo – and one directed at the international community, promising peace and stability in the region, with a steady flow of gas, oil and other raw materials – that is, preserving the status quo. It is obvious how any attempt to fulfil either one of the two promises renders impossible the fulfilment of the other.

Therefore, throughout most of the twentieth century, modern Arab states were seen as vassal states of the superpower of their day, whether this was Great Britain and France in the first half of the twentieth century or the United States in the second half. The Cold War provided an illusion of independence, as superpower rivalry provided Third World countries with some breathing space. Socialism also presented the intellectual Arab elites with a form of modernity that was seemingly anti-colonial. Hence Arab communist and socialist parties could oscillate between arguing that modern Arab nation-states were colonial cages to be destroyed and arguing that these same states could be temporarily considered as vehicles of modernisation and progress until they were dissolved in a larger pan-Arab entity.

After the Cold War, however, this breathing space vanished. During the Gulf War of 1990–91, when the United States and its allies came to the aid of Kuwait against Iraq, the 'new world order' meant that hundreds of thousands of American and allied troops were in the Arabian desert protecting the 'old world order': the colonial borders drawn by the British in the sands of Iraq and the Gulf after the First World War. The classic colonial mechanisms from the early twentieth century were back in place, with most Arab states now unquestionably vassals of the United States. Like feudal lords, their vassalage was the reason and precondition for their lordly titles. They were crying sovereignty to their own populations and pledging allegiance to the United States, trying to keep both legitimacy and recognition; the more they got of one the more they lost of the other.

Examples of such vassalage from the first half of the twentieth century include the Hussein–McMahon correspondence during the First World War, discussed by Avi Shlaim in this volume, the February declaration of 1922 by which Britain granted Egypt nominal independence, the 1936 'friendship and alliance' treaty between Egypt and Britain, and the Anglo-Iraqi treaty of 1931. Examples from the second half include the Camp David Accords between Egypt and Israel in

1978, and the many treaties signed during the seemingly endless peace process between Israel and the Palestine Liberation Organisation since 1993.

With the invasion of Iraq in 2003, all faith was lost in the ability of the modern, colonially created Arab nation-state. The compromise by which Arabs were to preserve colonial interests in return for nominal independence was shaken, as the United States resorted to classical conquest and direct rule. The modern state, with the modern army at its core, was shown to be utterly impotent in the face of its colonial creators. The Iraqi army could not protect the Iraqis against the Americans, and, by example, it was clear that the Egyptian army, if faced with the same challenge, would fail to protect the Egyptian people, and so on. Therefore, instead of these states, new forms of political organisation have emerged. Web-like entities, networks whose central node is a cloud of ideas and narratives, float across the region through word of mouth, poetry, music, religious sermons and news bulletins. People exposed to these narratives respond and act, without any central command. The networks thus can form and dissolve as needed. Here, narrative replaces structure, conviction replaces command, and improvisation from the margins replaces central planning. This has been a fundamental characteristic of the recent uprisings in the Middle East. Such non-state, non-hierarchical forms of organisation seem to provide society with an alternative to the formal, hierarchic, pyramid-like state structures and the system of centralised political parties, whether in power or in opposition.

If we look at Egypt, in early January 2011 a narrative was floating through social media, satellite channels, mosques, churches, universities, schools, factories and street cafés stating that people in Egypt could emulate the Tunisian uprising. A sentence mimicking the way schoolboys answer oral exams was widely circulated in social media: 'In the name of God, most gracious, most merciful: the answer is Tunisia.' People exposed to this overwhelming narrative were not organised in any party. Instead they improvised their actions in cells of two and three and ten and twenty, and took to the streets. Without a leader or a central committee, their movements on the ground were nonetheless highly coordinated, harmonious and effective.

During the eighteen days of demonstrations, between 25 January and 11 February, the Egyptian army command estimated the number of demonstrators throughout the country to have been around 20 million. This is almost equal to the population of Syria, twice the population of Tunisia, three times the population of Jordan or Palestine, five times the population of Lebanon and almost twenty times the population of Bahrain. Even if the numbers were at times exaggerated, these demonstrations would still be the largest in recorded Egyptian history. Yet these large numbers of people were able to manage communication, supply, information, security, defence and negotiation, without any ministries, committees, parties, or any other hierarchical centralised governing body, for eighteen days. They were able to improvise a social contract, an unwritten constitution, where relations between Muslims and Christians, Islamists and secularists, rich and poor, men and women, were more disciplined and amiable than they usually were under the rule of formal law. They were behaving as if they had a government, but without one. Leaders of political parties negotiating with the authorities found they could not lead the masses in the streets. In fact, it was the other way around; when public opinion in Tahrir Square was to continue the sit-in until Mubarak resigned, no conservative party could convince the masses to leave, and when the people decided to leave after Mubarak's resignation, no radical party could convince them to stay. The idea, the narrative and the public will had replaced both the state and the classic opposition. And that narrative was as clearly pro-democracy as it was anti-colonial. The latter is evidenced by a range of occurrences from anti-American and anti-Israeli slogans to the fact that the only embassy that came under attack in Egypt by angry demonstrators in 2011 was the Israeli embassy.

The country survived without a police force, which was destroyed on 28 January 2011, for almost five months. Only in May did the police start appearing again in Egypt, and that was only in Cairo, under the protection of the military. (Indicatively, their first appearance was to protect the Israeli embassy from demonstrators commemorating the Nakba, the loss of

Palestine and the foundation of Israel, on 15 May.) In the rest of the country, the police appeared much later. In the absence of the hard-core of the state, the military and the police, the country still functioned; society could manage well enough without the state. In the current struggle, after the coup d'état of July 2013, the state is trying to regain its power over an increasingly rebellious and independent society.

Yet, not every narrative is benevolent or benign. In societies divided by ethnic and religious rivalries, the fading away of state power, as might be expected, results in civil war. In Tunisia and Egypt in 2011 a degree of social consensus thwarted attempts by Ben Ali and Mubarak to split the narrative of the opposition, or to create rival narratives depicting the uprising as conspiracies by local Islamists or foreign agents. In Libya the situation was different. There the dilution of state power gave rise to conflicting narratives and warring identities. Gaddafi and his sons stressed that civil war would break out if their authority was lost or even diminished. The violent crackdown on dissenters deepened old tribal/provincial rivalries and created new ones. Civil war became a self-fulfilling prophecy. Since society, along with its narratives and identities, was the alternative to the state, the state actively worked for the disruption of society and the widening of the gaps among various subgroups within it. The state would smear the hands of its supporters with the blood of its opponents; that blood feud would subject the supporters to the existential fear of the opposition's revenge once it reached power; defending the state thus became a matter of self-preservation.

The Egyptian government that came to power after the July 2013 coup d'état also worked by this strategy of divide and rule. By committing massacres against opposition demonstrators in August 2014, in which hundreds (in some estimates, thousands) of men, women and children lost their lives, the government was creating a blood feud between various political factions and cultural groups within Egyptian society, thus making civil war more likely. Official government discourse then stressed the necessity of 'protecting the state' and 'supporting the president' because civil war was said to be the alternative. As the failure of the Arab colonially created nation-state drives society to escape its grip, the state actively attempts to sabotage such an escape, along with the potential for peaceful coexistence among society's various components.

While, in theory this strategy could save the state as an alternative to civil war, in practice it failed, as is clear in the cases of Libya, Syria, Iraq and Yemen. Instead of consolidating state power and showing society to be divided and weak, the state loses its authority ever more rapidly and more violently. Instead of losing its power to a unified social movement with a unifying narrative, it loses it to a number of armed militias, each with its own identity and narrative.

In Iraq the regular Iraqi army could not defend the country against the American invasion. The modern nation-state of Iraq, whose borders were drawn by the British Mandate authorities after the First World War, had failed to protect its own existence. In fact, it could be argued that its defeat was inevitable. An Iraqi victory against the neo-colonial campaigns of the United States would have required an advanced industrial base to produce a military more efficient than the combined forces of the US, the UK and their allies. But the modern Iraqi state was built by its British colonial designers as a relatively small oil-dependent rentier state with identity and legitimacy problems. One could argue, even, that precisely because Iraq was a state, precisely because its fighting force was organised in the form of a modern centralised army, it was bound to be defeated.

On the other hand, the myriad Iraqi decentralised militias inflicted enough losses on the occupying American forces to stop Washington reaping the political fruits of its invasion. Many of these militias were made of improvised cells formed by individuals exposed to the cloud of anti-American narratives emanating from personal experience, word of mouth, mosques, satellite channels or the internet, but they were organisationally isolated from any one hierarchy or leadership. There was usually no line of command to break, no command and control centre to bomb and no irreplaceable leader to arrest or assassinate. While the foreignness, lack of legitimacy, dependence, rentierism, paranoia and centralisation of the modern state and its hovering above society guaranteed its military defeat, the nativeness of the improvised network-like entities, their organic emergence from and merger with society guaranteed their resilience. Here again, an Arab society was doing the state's job.

Yet when society replaces the fading state, it comes with its own problems: a society divided along ethnic or religious lines expresses such divisions and allows them to be exploited by any interested, local, regional or international power. While those militias managed to inflict more damage on the occupying forces than the Iraqi army did, they also tore down the very fabric of Iraqi coexistence and plunged the country into civil war.

The situation in Syria is more complicated. Due to Syria's geostrategic position and its international alliances, almost all major political actors in the world became involved in the Syrian crisis. The Syrian civil war has been correctly described as a miniature world war, where regional and international rivalries are fought through exploiting domestic sectarian and ethnic divides. With almost half of Syria's population displaced and hundreds of thousands killed, the Syrian civil war threatens to become the single most devastating human catastrophe in the region since the occupation of Iraq.

While advocates of centralised state power elsewhere in the region point to Syria as the catastrophe waiting to happen to them if they let society lead, the state's failure is nowhere as acutely and as painfully felt as it is in Syria. Instead of becoming the prize over which factions fight, the state in Syria became itself just one faction among many.

Nonetheless, the Syrian civil war, along with its offshoots in Iraq and Lebanon, cannot be won. Wars among communities of tens of millions, such as the Shiites and the Sunnis, are unwinnable. Despite the brutality, in time all factions will come to realise that no one can eliminate the other. The form of the new coexistence will then be dictated by the regional and international balance of power.

The threatening of the colonial order in the Middle East, and the state system created by this order, affects almost all Arab countries. The painful dismantling of Iraq, Syria, Libya, Yemen, Sudan and Lebanon are cases at hand; Algeria and Saudi Arabia might also face serious challenges in the near future. But I argue as well that the dismantling of the colonial system will certainly affect Israel more than any other country in the region. Israel will have to worry because, if narrative is replacing structure, if ethnic and religious identities are replacing state-based affiliations and if public opinion becomes a determining factor in Middle East politics, it will not be long before an anti-Israeli consensus, or quasi-consensus, manifests itself, even after taking the current sectarian conflicts into account.

It is much easier to end the military occupation of the West Bank and Gaza, or even change the Israeli law of return, and de-Zionise the state of Israel, than it is to end Sunnism or Shiism. Unlike sectarian wars, struggles against legal systems and political regimes are winnable. In fact, such struggles have often been won:

for example, the American civil rights movement or the struggle against apartheid in South Africa. Other than being morally wrong, wars against ethnic or religious communities of millions are impossible to win. In a Middle East where narratives and ideas increasingly determine both peaceful and violent political behaviour, the narrative around which consensus could be easily built is the Palestinian narrative. After all, Zionism is an ideology/political system that discriminates among people based on their religion; it is equally unfriendly to Arab Muslims, Christians, Shiites, Sunnis, Islamists or nationalists. If the 4 million Palestinian refugees were to become Jewish tomorrow, they would be allowed back to their homes with all the rights and privileges of citizenship. If the 3 million Palestinians living in the West Bank and Gaza were to become Jewish tomorrow, they would be given the chance to vote for or against the laws and military directives that have been governing their lives for the past forty-eight years. Even opportunistic politicians will realise that one way to end the civil war of narratives raging in the Middle East is by reintroducing a narrative around which there is consensus. A challenge to Israel may well turn the various civil wars into one major regional war.

To conclude, the colonially created Arab states are old cracked cauldrons filled with boiling narratives and passions that cannot be contained. The first searing streams of the boiling deluge are already spilling out of these cauldrons' cracks, and they may turn the region into a lake of fire soon. The future therefore looks grim and violent civil war may well turn into an international conflict involving Israel, the region and perhaps the superpowers. It is dark, yet out of that darkness there might be hope that new forms of political existence, new identities, new ideas and narratives, more responsive to people's rights and more effective in meeting people's needs than the nation-state, more inclusive than the tribe and the religious sect, might emerge.

## Postscript: A Poem

Given my themes, it is appropriate to sum up this essay with an excerpt from a poem I wrote in the summer of 2014.

### It Was Not Wise
(translated into English verse by the author)

*It was not wise of you, O Death, to come so close*
*It was not wise of you to place us under siege*
*For you to camp year after year so near our homes*
*So often have we met, we've memorised your face*
*We've come to know when you prefer to have your meals*
*Your sleeping times, your temper and your shifting moods*
*Your heart's desires and your hidden weaknesses*
*We know you well, O long-time neighbour, so beware*
*And please do not feel safe that you have counted us*
*For we are more than you can count, and more than you*
*For more than sixty years of war we've held our ground*

*For two millennia many Christs have walked these hills*
*Like schoolboys bearing unseen crosses on their backs*
*And lamps still shine in what remains of homes destroyed*
*How many times will you repeat yourself to us?*
*It's boring, as we must repeat ourselves to you*
*There is no death, but fear of death, and since that's gone*
        *...*
*Be sure, our old-time neighbour, we will have you killed*
*So, Death! know this: next time you're minded to Crusade*
*Fear us, for out of boredom, we won't be afraid.*

# A LONG VIEW FROM BAGHDAD

## Justin Marozzi

ARE HISTORIANS any guide to the future? Answering with my historian's hat on, I feel that it's a bit like the caliph asking a eunuch to sample his harem of concubines. You'd love to do it, but you're just not sure you've got the right equipment. As historians we deal in the past – it's what we immerse ourselves in professionally, for years on end – and it's surely only right to be suitably humble about the predictive powers of a subject that looks backwards rather than forwards.

I remember in the immediate run-up to the Iraq War of 2003 the *Guardian* published a survey of views on the impending conflict from leading historians on both sides of the Atlantic. Though the verdicts were varied, the weight of opinion, as you would expect from the *Guardian*, was anti-war. Most disputed the historical analogies made by both the pro-war (this was Munich 1938) and the anti-war (no, it was Suez 1956) camps. The Bush and Blair governments portrayed anti-war opinion as the appeasement of a dangerous dictator who threatened world peace. A number of their opponents predicted the looming conflict would be another Suez, an imperial fiasco revisited.

'History never repeats itself, ever. That's its murderous charm,' Simon Schama argued. 'The poet Joseph Brodsky, in his great essay "A Profile of Clio", wrote that when history comes, it always takes you by surprise, and that's what I believe, too.' Having said that, Schama then went on to predict that Western-led war in Iraq would bring a chaotic and broken state, 'a teddy bears' picnic for terrorism'.[1] It is difficult, looking back from the vantage point of 2015, to argue with that. In fact, it was a remarkably prescient forecast from a man who believed history was a series of surprises.

Before discussing the turmoil raging across Iraq and Syria, let's go back to the eighth century for a dose of historical enlightenment. The year was 775 and the founder of Baghdad, the Abbasid caliph Abu Jaafar al Mansur, 'The Victorious', had just died. He had left strict instructions to his son and heir, Mahdi, and his daughter-in-law, Rita, together with a key to a door that must not be opened until his death was confirmed. Off trooped Mahdi and his wife, expecting to find an underground storeroom full of treasures: gold, precious stones and so on. The wealth of the world had been piling up in Baghdad during the past decade, since the city's foundation in 762, and already it was becoming the cultural, commercial and political capital of the planet.

But instead, when Mahdi and Rita opened the door, they found an entire storeroom full of dead bodies. Men, women and children of all ages, and every single one of them had a little leather tag in their ear detailing the name, the tribe and the exact genealogy of the victim. The one thing that they had in common was that every single one of them was an Alid, a supporter of Ali, the Prophet Muhammad's cousin and son-in-law. In a word, a Shia.

The reason why I tell that story is not to cast a little note of cheer into the prevailing Middle Eastern gloom, as much as we all need it, but to make the point that the sectarian tensions that bedevil the region today have existed in Iraq since Baghdad was founded in the late eighth century. These sectarian tensions, in other words, are not a creation of the Americans or the British, much as they may have exacerbated them. That is the first thing, I would argue, that we should bear in mind when we discuss Iraq in the twenty-first century. And the second is that for almost its entire history – with only a brief hiccup in the tenth and eleventh centuries under the Shia Buyid dynasty and a fleeting glimpse of Safavid rule in the seventeenth – Iraq has always been ruled by a Sunni minority. That was the ancient structure of power the US and the UK overturned in 2003, with consequences that we still live with – and Iraqis die from in their droves today.

I must stress that this is not the same thing as saying Iraq is a country where Sunni and Shia cannot and do not live quite happily together. The vast majority of Iraqis, for a large portion of their history, have done precisely that, whether in the glorious times of the Abbasid caliphate or during the era of nationalism, pan-Arabism and Baathism a thousand years later. Peaceful coexistence tends not to make headlines in the same way that explosive violence does. What has changed during the past decade from 2003 is the sharp polarisation between the communities and the redrawing of the sectarian map of Baghdad, which has been transformed from a mixed city to a largely Shia city with Sunni enclaves.

It is a fact that Shia rule in Iraq remains unacceptable today to many Sunnis – and vice versa. There is no shortage of Sunni aristocrats, including highly educated friends of mine who helped me when I was researching my history of Baghdad, who flatly deny that the Shia are a majority in Iraq. Some Sunnis I have spoken to see the Shia as peasants, barbarians, uneducated, illiterate, unfit to be the natural rulers of Iraq. They describe them in terms better excluded from these pages. It is an extreme view, certainly, but it is surprisingly widely held. It is also, perhaps, typical of an urban–rural divide which characterises much of the region, indeed much of the world.

If that sets the scene in terms of a brief demographic portrait of Iraq, we should also take note of how the territory was administered in the days before it became a modern nation-state, headed by a new Hashemite monarch, King Faisal I, in 1921. When Sultan Suleiman the Magnificent arrived before the city walls and took Baghdad in 1534, he ushered in a lengthy era of Ottoman control that lasted until the British arrived in 1917. (Unlike many other conquerors, including his Ottoman predecessor, aptly named Salim the Grim, he offered respect to both Sunni and Shia subjects, making pilgrimages to important Shia shrines.) One could argue that the Turks, co-religionists of the Iraqi people, understood the place rather better than the British in the twentieth century and the Americans in the twenty-first. For one thing the Ottomans ran what later became Iraq as three *vilayets*, or provinces. To generalise about these three regions, Mosul in the north was largely but not exclusively Kurdish, Baghdad in the centre was largely but not exclusively Sunni, and Basra in the south was predominantly Shia with exceptions. The Ottomans, in other words, chose to administer this territory as three related but separate provinces. The British, in their wisdom, decided to throw them all together and create the new state of Iraq.

Being British in design, the new state naturally had to have a king. When assessing how successful was the monarchy, we can begin with a reflection on its relatively brief duration. Created with high hopes in 1921, it ended in a hail of bullets in Baghdad in 1958. Though some Iraqis look back to this as a halcyon period of Iraq's history and a rare time of stability, it should be noted that within fifteen years of King Faisal's coronation Baghdad earned the dubious distinction of hosting the first coup within the modern Middle East when General Bakr Sidki replaced the civilian government with a military regime in 1936. If we are looking for constancy under the British Mandate and in pre-revolutionary Iraq, the dominant figure of his time was unquestionably Nuri Pasha, who generally occupied the positions of foreign minister or defence minister when he was not serving one of eight terms as prime minister. First appointed premier in 1930, he survived as a minister until 1958, when he too came to a bloody end. He, like so many of his governments, was viewed by many Iraqis as a British stooge. In the era of Nasser, it was hardly surprising that nationalism and pan-Arabism found fertile soil in Iraq from the 1950s. To summarise the period from the creation of Iraq to the rise of the Baathists, we could do worse than recall the forgivably jaundiced words of King Faisal shortly before his death in 1933: 'In Iraq, there is still – and I say this with a heart full of sorrow – no Iraqi people but unimaginable masses of human beings, devoid of any patriotic idea, imbued with religious traditions and absurdities, connected by no common tie, giving ear to evil, prone to anarchy, and perpetually ready to rise against any government whatever.'[2]

On the one hand, then, you have Iraq or Meso-potamia as home to the world's oldest civilisation, with successive empires flourishing in the fertile Land Between the Rivers from Sumerian times in the sixth millennium BC through the Babylonian, Assyrian, Achaemenid, Seleucid, Parthian, Roman and Sassanid periods. On the other, you have Iraq as a modern nation-state with limited history – less than a century old and with serious questions now being asked about its very future as a nation-state. I have had numerous conversations with Iraqis discussing the possibilities of an Iraqi break-up, including its fracturing into three parts along ethnic and sectarian lines: a 'Sunnistan' in central Iraq, with a Kurdistan to the north and a 'Shia-stan' to the south. For more encouraging signs that Iraq may weather its latest storm and remain a sovereign state, a recent survey found that although 81 per cent of Sunnis and just 34 per cent of Shia favoured a separation of religion and politics, 'both Sunni and Shia tended to identify themselves as Iraqis rather than as Muslims or Arabs'.[3] Whatever their positions, few take the survival of Iraq with its present borders for granted.

So much for that brief survey of Iraq's demographics and earlier methods of administration. If we are to understand the ongoing crisis in Iraq – not to mention that in Syria, Egypt, Yemen and Libya – it is essential to give some thought to the quality of government and governance. I would argue that in recent years Iraq has suffered terribly from a devastating lack of good governance. Iraqis of a certain age – sophisticated urban Sunnis especially – go misty-eyed when discussing the 1950s, which they see as the last of the halcyon days in the country. It was a time of peace, rising prosperity, a vibrant cultural life, architectural innovation and growing regional influence. Tragically, it proved all too short-lived. With the revolution of 1958, the British-supported monarchy met its bloody end and Iraq became a republic. Instead of leading to greater freedoms and a more inclusive politics, however, the 1960s deteriorated quickly from hope to despair – and violence between Communists, Baathists and pan-Arabists. General Abd al Karim Kassem, leader of the revolution and champion of the Iraqi masses, was himself executed in 1963 by his former comrade in arms Colonel Abdusalam Aref. Power was not to be shared. It was to be won – and preserved at all costs – by force.

Recent decades have certainly contributed to the crisis that we see now in Iraq. A certain form of political stability, one could argue, arrived with Saddam Hussein seizing complete power in 1979 – having ruthlessly taken charge of the various intelligence and security agencies during the previous decade (as did, more recently, the former prime minister Nouri al-Maliki during his eight years as premier). But at what a cost! Very shortly after taking power, Saddam launched a war against Iran. That lasted a decade, and the casualty count was between 1 million and 1.5 million on both sides. Complete ruin and apocalypse for both countries.

Within two years of that war ending, Saddam precipitated the first Gulf War in 1990, when, in American Secretary of State James Baker's words, issued as a pre-war threat, Iraq was bombed 'back into the Stone Age'.[4] Iraqis haven't really known peace and its dividends since that time. The 1990s were an appalling decade, when Iraqis bled under UN Security Council sanctions while Saddam and his entourage got richer. Infant malnutrition became endemic in a country that should have been prospering from oil revenues. UNICEF estimated around 500,000 children under five died unnecessarily as a result of the embargo.[5] Visiting Baghdad in the 1990s, the Canadian writer Paul Roberts aptly described what had been happening to Iraq during the past twenty years as 'a psychological holocaust'.[6] Bear in mind what has happened to Iraq *since* the 1990s.

Sanctions only ended in 2003 with the US-led invasion, which quickly triggered an al-Qaeda-led insurgency of unfathomable violence, drawing in disgruntled Baathists and a shifting mix of tribal militias. Living in Baghdad at that time, I was sometimes shaken out of bed by yet another car bomb blowing innocent Iraqis to smithereens. It always used to amaze me – and still does – that the flow of young men prepared to kill themselves in a jihad which took almost exclusively Muslim blood was apparently so endless.

From al-Qaeda it was only a short, bloody step – via the deeply corrupt, incompetent and sectarian premiership of Nouri al-Maliki – to ISIL (Daesh in Arabic) today. And now we find ourselves in yet another bloody Iraqi crisis. For the first time in 2,000 years the ancient city of Mosul has no Christians. Yazidis have been butchered. Iraqi Jews have already been hounded into extinction, suffering the same fate as their co-religionists across so much of the Middle East. It is one of many tragedies that corruption in the

Iraqi army is so bad that vast swathes of the country have fallen to the jihadists as army units, neglected by their commanding officers, starved of proper supplies of food, water and equipment, have simply melted away.

The point of that summary of Iraq's recent history is to emphasise the calamitous lack of good governance that has bedevilled the country in recent decades and which continues to do so. Good governance in Iraq – and across much of the Middle East – is an oxymoron. This is not simply the view of another critical Westerner. Go back to the UNDP's Arab Human Development Report of 2002, compiled by a team of Arab scholars, and review some of its key findings. That inaugural report highlighted what it called three major deficits at the heart of the Arab world's predicament – in freedom, knowledge and women's empowerment. 'The transfer of power through the ballot box is not a common phenomenon in the Arab world,' the report noted in a triumph of understatement. As for the quality of education on offer, as Imam Ali bin Abi Taleb wrote in the seventh century, 'If God were to humiliate a human being, He would deny him knowledge.' On the question of women's position in Arab societies, where the report was more hopeful, the rise of Daesh in Syria and Iraq, and the growing conservatism of a number of countries, does not augur well. As Iraqis know only too well, you cannot enjoy peaceful development, basic public services, human rights, a functioning economy and an inclusive political environment if your leaders are unwilling or unable to share political power equitably on the one hand and guarantee security on the other.

When you look at the Arab Spring, in Iraq it seems to me it never really happened. It is surely one of the greatest tragedies for the Arab world that the hope unleashed by popular movements across the region, from Tunisia, Egypt and Libya to Syria and Bahrain, has been so comprehensively snuffed out – with the single exception of Tunisia. In Egypt vested interests in the army hit the default button, protecting their economic interests, imprisoning opponents and dealing a near death blow to democratic forces. In Libya, militias have refused to disarm, tribal and regional differences have been allowed to intensify and foreign powers have boosted Islamist extremists in the east of the country, making peace and stability a more distant prospect than ever. You now have two premiers and two 'governments' in two cities. It wasn't meant to be like this. Looking at Syria in early 2015, it is difficult to see that vicious conflict ending any time soon. Summarising things crudely, you have a cruel dictator versus vicious Islamists, with the moderate opposition squeezed into virtual irrelevance for the time being. The cynical words of Henry Kissinger, when describing the Iraq–Iran War, spring to mind: 'A pity they both can't lose.' But, as is always the case in war, it is the ordinary people who are losing everything.

The only consolation I can take from this desperately bleak picture in Iraq and across the region – once more with a historian's hat on – is that it takes time to recover from devastating dictatorships and prolonged conflict. Gaddafi ruled – and eviscerated – Libya for forty-three years. As I write, it has been less than four years since his removal. It may take a generation to recover, and of course there is no guarantee of a happy ending. I always felt, having worked in Libya since the 1980s, that if Libya couldn't make a decent fist of the Arab Spring, no country could. Rich in energy resources, with a small and moderate population and no sectarian divide, Libya is favourably blessed. Yet the turmoil there continues.

As a natural optimist I've found the events of the past few years, especially in Iraq, Syria, Egypt and Libya, profoundly disheartening. One thing I've learned from studying thirteen centuries of Iraqi history is that turbulence and conflict are almost the norm. Stability tends to be elusive. Of course Sunni and Shia can live together very happily, and they generally do, together with Jews and Christians, but all too often there are these extraordinarily violent flashpoints, frequently exacerbated by foreign invasions, a recurrent curse in the history of the Middle East. I remember years ago one of my Middle East history professors likened the Western powers to quarrelling dinosaurs. As they fought in Europe, their long tails would sweep across the Middle East, destroying countries, remaking borders and creating new facts on the ground that the local population then had to live with. Has anything changed, I wonder, as we contemplate more Western intervention in Iraq and Syria?

There is an ongoing debate about whether the West should intervene militarily in Iraq and Syria. In a 2014 piece in the *Spectator* advocating robust military intervention, I was fascinated – OK, horrified – to read that one of the reasons given by the writer was that the new Iraqi prime minister, Haider al-Abadi, speaks fluent English and has a DPhil from the University of Manchester. The message was clear. He's one of us, so it'll all be all right. Then came the argument that the American failure was not to have spent too long in Iraq but to have left too early – after eight years. To me that argument is complete fantasy, as good an example as any of the lack of understanding of Middle Eastern history, politics and culture. I would suggest that we in the West should be much more humble and realistic about what we can achieve in the Middle East and acknowledge what general publics in both the West and Middle East know only too well, especially after the case studies of Iraq and Afghanistan: we're not very good at interventions.

Looking ahead, I think that in fifteen years Iraq will be a violent, difficult place. Some Iraqis say its best hope may well be under someone who is able to create security, and in recent years that has tended to mean a strongman or dictator. Against that dispiriting view, one should also note that a recent survey found that 88 per cent of Iraqis considered democracy the best form of governance for Iraq – in which case politicians and the population will need to learn and put into practice some of its basic principles, from transparent government and the protection of minorities to honest elections and the peaceful transfer of power.[7] Iraq should be one of the most prosperous countries in the world, but it's not. It's sitting on a lake of oil, but can barely get the oil out of the ground. Iraqis have seen so much warfare, but it's proving incredibly difficult for them to return to anything approaching a peaceful situation. Politicians urgently need to provide responsible, non-sectarian leadership and functioning public services.

The name of Baghdad is City of Peace – Madinat al-Salaam – and one reason why we might be optimistic is that this is a city that has withstood everything history has thrown at it over the centuries. It has been invaded by Genghis Khan's grandson Hulagu, by Tamerlane, the Ottomans, the Persians, the Americans, the British and most recently by al-Qaeda, yet still the city survives. But it is a pale shadow of its former self. It used to be the greatest city in the world, a magnet for some of the most brilliant minds from Central Asia to the Atlantic coast, but now, sadly, there has been a colossal brain drain. The middle classes have been decimated, sent into exile, slaughtered. It's a city still suffering a psychological holocaust, that term used back in the 1990s.

If we're talking about the economic empowerment of the region, this is very closely tied to political development. If good governance and a more democratic or more inclusive, power-sharing system of rule can take root in the region, it's not going to be introduced by American tanks or British Tornados. Iraqis – and Arabs – are going to have to seize their destiny themselves – and be allowed to do so.

We humans are a forward-looking species and because it's important to remain as optimistic as possible in these dark and difficult times I'm going to end with the words of my great Iraqi friend and collaborator Manaf al-Damluji, who now lives in exile in the US, having been driven out of Iraq by the raging violence of recent years: 'The cycle that sees Baghdad lurching between mayhem and prosperity has been long and gory, but of course we must have hope. May the City of Peace live up to its name before we ourselves depart to eternal peace.'

# IRAN: COMING IN FROM THE COLD?

**Ramita Navai**

THE ISLAMIC REPUBLIC OF IRAN likes to look lonely. It prides itself on being a fortress in a hostile world, encircled by truculent Arab nations and an aggressive Israel that is always ready to pounce. This partly stems from a culture of victimhood deep in the Iranian psyche – that of the oppressed Shia, forever marginalised, forever the underdog. But it is also a function of Iran and Iranians being demonised by the West. Isolated internationally, the Islamic Republic has learned to survive on its own. A regime ideology of standing alone against enemies has been forged and tempered in wars of one kind or another, whether the hot and bloody conflict with Iraq, which cost over a million Iranian and Iraqi lives, or the newer cold conflict of sanctions and diplomatic seclusion. This status of the isolated outcast has allowed the regime to ramp up the revolutionary rhetoric and externalise blame for its internal frailties.

But now it seems Iran has grown weary of isolation.

It wants to come in from the cold. What better moment than when the region is threatened with serial crises, dangerous wars and instability than to evoke the image of Iran as the moderate regional broker that the West can do business with? The Arab Spring and the unravelling of the Middle East that followed have provided Tehran with unprecedented opportunities to expand its regional and international influence, and perhaps to draw the sting from a growing domestic opposition.

The cries for reform and the gunfire that met and killed protesters back in 2009 during mass protests against the theocratic regime still resonate today. Six years ago, millions of Iranians took to the streets to contest the latest presidential election results. The regime had been blindsided and it responded with lightning brutality. Hundreds were killed; thousands were imprisoned. The government appeared panicky – even turning on its own, among them some of the founding figures and architects of the Islamic Republic itself. The presidential candidates and leaders of the so-called reformist Green Movement, Mir Hossein Mousavi and the cleric Mehdi Karroubi, were placed under house arrest. A feeling of overwhelming anger and resentment gripped the country. Even some members of the Basij militia, the paramilitary volunteer organisation operating throughout the country, showed disgust at government violence, refusing orders to beat demonstrators. The regime had never appeared so factious and vulnerable.

When the Arab Spring began just over a year

later, some say triggered by the 2009 protests, in true regime-style the Islamic Republic tried to appropriate the uprisings, calling them an 'Islamic Awakening' and spinning the protests as populist support for Islam against imperialism and oppression. Tehran feared that the rebellions would inspire the Green Movement to rise up again. The regime moved fast by snatching another opportunity to invoke revolutionary ideology – the state's predictable and incessant need to reinforce its own raison d'être: it compared the Arab Spring to the Islamic revolution. This rebranding of the Arab Spring as part of the tradition of Iran's revolution did not work. But the results of the Arab Spring's drift into a chaotic and bitter winter of counter-revolution and civil war meant that even opponents of Iran's regime backed away from the notion of a wider movement towards reform in the Islamic Middle East. In addition, Iran drew some satisfaction with what appeared to be a rapid decline in the influence of the Great Satan, the United States, over many of Washington's former client states and allies in Cairo, Jeddah, the UAE and North Africa. However, Iran's influence, at least initially, also looked to be diminishing.

The Syrian civil war cemented the divide between Iran, a Shia nation, and the Arab world, mostly Sunni, which viewed Iran as a menacing interloper in the Syrian crisis. Iran has been the main sponsor of the Assad regime ever since the collapse of its original benefactor, the Soviet Union. As Iran's only real ally in the region, Syria is of supreme geopolitical and strategic importance to Iran; with a shared hatred of the United States and Israel (and initially a shared hatred of Saddam Hussein's Iraq), Syria forms a key part of the 'axis of resistance' challenging what Iranians perceive to be US ambitions of regional hegemony. Syria also acts as a Shia-friendly buffer to anti-Iranian Sunni countries. If Assad falls and the majority Sunnis take power in Syria, the so-called 'Shia crescent' that stretches from Tehran, slicing through Iraq and Syria into southern Lebanon, will be broken. Iran would also lose its main means of pressurising Israel, because a Sunni or Western-installed government would not allow the regime to supply weaponry to the Lebanese Shia militias of Hezbullah through its borders (as Assad has been doing).

To ensure Assad's survival, Iran sent weapons and fuel. The Revolutionary Guard Corps dispatched hundreds of men, including senior commanders from the elite Qods Force, to train and advise Syrian government forces. Syria quickly became the battle-ground for proxy wars, with Shia Iran pitted against old enemies in the form of Saudi- and Gulf-funded Sunni jihadists and militias. As the effects of the war spilled over into neighbouring countries, there was a backlash against Iranian meddling in Lebanon. When Iraq crumbled under the divisive Iranian-supported president, Nouri al-Maliki, who had inflamed political sectarian divisions, alienating Sunnis and Kurds as he destroyed national institutions and the army as threats to his Shia rule, Iran was blamed.

More worryingly for those in power, resentment against the Iranian regime was spreading at home in the early stages of the Syrian civil war. Post-2009, Iranians were finding it increasingly hard to swallow the regime's bellicose and theocratic revolutionary propaganda. After a disastrous eight years in office, President Mahmoud Ahmadinejad left the country in a mess. The economy was in ruins, with inflation at about 40 per cent and the rial the lowest it has been against the dollar in decades. Iranians were subjected to debilitating sanctions imposed by the United Nations, the US and the European Union over its nuclear programme. News of the regime reportedly spending billions of dollars on the internecine Syrian war did not go down well with the public.

When President Hassan Rouhani was elected in 2013, his speeches on equal women's rights and social equity ignited hope. During his campaign, he had used the symbol of a key to represent the unlocking of the political door, inferring that once open he would rescue both the economy and civil society. But almost immediately, citizens' rights and the struggle for a more robust civil society fell victim to the internal battle between the reformists and the hardliners. Life for ordinary Iranians has not changed much under Rouhani.

Just as President Khatami experienced during his term, most of Rouhani's attempts at social reform were stifled by the country's hardliners. Keen to reassure conservative supporters that they are still in charge, these hardliners have ensured that morality police patrols continue. There are the same periodical crack-downs on women deemed to be wearing 'bad hijab' – from an awry or too transparent scarf to form-fitting clothing. Women have been banned from volleyball matches at the Azadi stadium in Tehran and a British-Iranian national was imprisoned for daring to attend a match in protest – a very loud and clear signal intended to embarrass Rouhani, who was in the midst of negotiating with the British on the nuclear issue. The conservatives, as usual, revel in controlling all aspects of women's sexuality, absurdly spending valuable time in parliament discussing 'leggings' – not, as one would hope, as a crime against fashion, but as a crime against morality.

Iran's human rights record has regressed. According to the United Nations, there has been an 'alarming' surge in executions, with over 800 prisoners killed in Rouhani's first year in office.[1] Iran's most famous political prisoners, Mousavi and Karroubi, are still under house arrest. Other victims of the power struggle between Rouhani's administration and the hardline-controlled judiciary and intelligence ministry were journalists and activists. With at least thirty journalists imprisoned in 2014, according to the Committee to Protect Journalists, Iran ranked second to China as the world's biggest jailer of journalists. The *Washington Post*'s Tehran correspondent, Jason Rezaian, an Iranian-American, was arrested even as Iran was negotiating with the US. He has been detained for longer than any other Western journalist in the country.

The hardliners know they must strike a careful

balance between reminding their citizens of the red lines and keeping them sweet. They are very aware that they can no longer stop information from the West coming in. News channels, Western films and porn are all beamed into the country via satellite dishes bought on the black market and installed in the houses of all classes, secular and religious alike, over the whole of Iran. A government official recently acknowledged that there were around 4.5 million satellite receivers in the country. Despite heavy censorship of the internet – dubbed the 'Filternet' – the government has reported that nearly 70 per cent of the 23.5 million young people using the internet deploy proxy servers called VPNs – Virtual Private Networks – to circumvent the government's internet filter, allowing computers to function as if they were in another country.[2] During elections and protests, the authorities grind internet connections down to an excruciatingly slow speed. The internet has also spawned new social trends that threaten the fundamental values of the Islamic state. More and more people are using dating and hook-up sites that provide opportunities for 'un-Islamic' meetings; the internet has also invigorated the gay scene. According to recent figures released by Google, internet searches for porn in Iran are reportedly one of the highest in the world.[3] In response, the government launched the cyberpolice in 2011 to fight internet crimes and protect 'national and religious identity'. The cyberpolice have also announced crackdowns on internet and Facebook pages that promote pornography and prostitution.

As economic conditions worsen due to stifling sanctions and economic mismanagement and corruption under Ahmadinejad, so do societal problems. And with increasing access to information, these are getting harder to shield from view. Iran now has one of the highest rates of drug addiction in the world. Official estimates of the number of addicts varies wildly – between 1 and 3 million – and crystal methamphetamine has now overtaken heroin to become the second drug of choice, after opium. Drug addiction among women has reportedly doubled in the past couple of years. The government has launched anti-drug advertising campaigns and there are drug rehabilitation centres. Despite the failing economy, the illegal narcotics trade is booming.

Prostitution has become so ubiquitous on the streets of Tehran that the issue has been discussed in parliament over the past years. Official figures of prostitutes in Tehran are at around 300,000, which many believe is an underestimate, with the average age of girls starting out only sixteen. The interior ministry has even suggested rounding the women up and taking them to a specially designated camp where they can be 'reformed'. Material need seems to be eroding the moral high ground so vigorously and often viciously touted by the regime.

On a winter's day in late 2013, on a busy main road in Tehran, a dozen women are touting for business; among them is a housewife whose husband has lost his job and a student from a southern province. There are fewer women than usual, as recent raids have forced most of the women to work from a shopping mall a few blocks away. Here the women are younger and some admit they are not driven by a need for financial survival but by a need for conspicuous consumption.

'I pick out whatever I want – usually clothes or handbags – and the client will buy them. And then we'll go to his place and have sex,' says one prostitute in her early twenties, whose wages as a secretary do not cover luxury items. She says she feels a sense of satisfaction in selling sex, because in her own way she is making a political stand.

Attitudes to sex are changing across society. Among some groups, sex has become a form of rebellion, where those who feel constrained by the social strictures of the regime say that only in sex do they feel that they have absolute control over their bodies and lives.

Disillusionment and discontent thus bubble to the surface; Rouhani and other pragmatic politicians realise that the status quo is precarious and cannot be maintained for ever. Despite Rouhani's stirring statements on the freedom of the press and civil rights, he has not been able to deliver on these issues. If he fails he will at best be cast in the same mould as Khatami – a weak president unable to get political traction and placate the hardliners. At worst, his failure to turn the economy around could be the catalyst for another uprising.

Rouhani's reaction has been to concentrate all his efforts on solving Iran's nuclear crisis; if he can negotiate with the West and have sanctions eased, he can unlock the key to inevitable reform through economic growth and relations with the outside world. Sanctions are not new to Iran. They started when the US froze Iran's assets during the hostage crisis over thirty years ago, but with the plummeting price of oil in 2015 and exports slashed to a third under Ahmedinejad, the results have been catastrophic for average Iranians, who have seen the value of their wages plummet.

However, the nuclear negotiations have already dragged on for twelve years. Iran insists it simply wants nuclear power, while the West and Israel maintain it wants a bomb. The nuclear programme is one of the few issues that unifies Iranians of all political and social stripes. It elicits a passionate response born not only from pride – the patriotism of national identity – but also from a sense of injustice at Western hypocrisy. Even Iranians opposed to the Islamic regime argue it is unfair that Iran is surrounded by nuclear powers such as Pakistan and Israel, all of which acquired nuclear programmes illegally, yet unlike Iran are not signatories to the nuclear non-proliferation treaty and are not subject to the same stringent scrutiny. The framework for a nuclear agreement set at Lausanne on 2 April 2015 cemented hope for a final deal. The foreign minister, Mohammed Javad Zarif, was even given a hero's welcome on his return to Tehran. Crucially, the Supreme Leader was careful to reign in criticism of the negotiations, giving Rouhani and his government room to manoeuvre. This was a clear indication that even in the higher echelons of the regime, making a deal with the Great Satan seemed necessary not only for economic recovery, but as part of a geo-political strategy.

Nevertheless, Rouhani is still meeting most resistance from hardliners over negotiations which focus on reducing the country's nuclear capabilities. Iranian hardliners see a nuclear Iran as non-negotiable. The day after the historic phone call between Rouhani and Obama on 27 September 2013, posters produced by the Revolutionary Guard sprang up across the city depicting two hands stretched out, ready to shake. One was Iranian, the other the clawed hand of the devil – the United States.

When Rouhani first came to power many thought he would be the perfect person to walk the tightrope between the technocrats and pragmatists (people like the powerful cleric and ex-president Rafsanjani) and the hardliners. But Rouhani is not an obvious liberal. For sixteen years he was the Supreme Leader's representative in the Supreme National Security Council, which has ultimate power in setting nuclear policy. He may have softened his position and be well placed to bring others with him. Yet even as an insider Rouhani has struggled to negotiate a clear policy. This shows just how much power the hardliners wield, and how much it probably suits them to keep Iran as a lonely pariah state.

Just when this attitude appeared to be driving Iran

into another stalemate with the international community, and as Iran's regional power appeared to be dwindling with the draining effects of sending men and arms to fight in Syria and Iraq, along came a perfect enemy: the Islamic State (IS). The apocalyptic Sunni death cult has provided the hardliners from within the regime with a new cause for war – and perhaps an opportunity for reformers to bring Iran in from the international cold.

The Islamic Republic has always striven to be seen as the superpower of the region and, for the first time since the 1979 revolution, the regime may be the closest it has ever been to fulfilling that dream. Iran, although still suffering from isolation, is now among the more stable countries in the Middle East. The chaos wreaked by the Islamic State, the disintegration of old alliances and the potential to redraw borders are kicking up opportunities – and Iran has thrust itself on to centre stage.

The regime is also enjoying a more submissive population, for there is less thirst for dramatic domestic regime change than ever before. This is partly a result of the government's brutal reaction to the 2009 protests and partly a result of the chaos raging in the countries across its borders – both of which have left Iranians feeling cautious and fearful. It is increasingly common to hear talk of change coming from within; even those who claim to abhor the regime seem resigned to slow, internal evolution. Unlike a decade ago, it is unusual to hear talk of outside intervention and of revolution.

: :

Suddenly, Tehran and Washington have found themselves on the same side, de facto (and unacknowledged) allies fighting a common threat. In late 2014, after a summer where the Islamic State swept through the border areas of both Iraq and Syria, the countries shared intelligence – although it must be remembered that it is not the first time this has happened. The Iranians shared intelligence with the US over the Taliban in 2001, and nothing came of that, so the question must be asked: can there be more than a temporary tactical union?

But Washington and Tehran may be drifting closer to one another on the winds of war that blow through Mesopotamia. After the downfall of Maliki and the ascension of a more acceptable Iraqi regime to both Washington and Tehran, Iran has provided troops, military advice and equipment to help the Iraqi army against the IS onslaught. Similarly, the US-led coalition has provided air support to fight the same enemy. American Special Forces and Iranian Quds soldiers have been sharing the same battle space on the ground as Iranian and American jets fly above them. Not talking directly, not even acknowledging each other's existence, but nonetheless comrades in arms against a common enemy.

Iran's engagement against the Islamic State has had a surprising effect at home: the Revolutionary Guards, who are usually viewed with suspicion and disdain, are being regarded with more respect; more and more Iranians are now proud that their forces are gaining the world's attention and fighting off an evil enemy. Even the tone of opinion pieces in reformist newspapers such as *Shargh* and *Etemaad* is much more supportive of and positive towards the Revolutionary Guards, and its commander, Qassem Suleimani, has become a heroic figure.

The rise of the Islamic State has also changed the game plan for nuclear negotiations. Détente with the West is key for Rouhani, not just in overcoming the hardliners, but in strengthening Iran's role in the region. A positive outcome to the nuclear negotiations would allow sanctions to be lifted and oil sales to recover and give Iran access to some $100 billion in frozen assets.

But the West needs resolution just as much as Rouhani. Before the emergence of the so-called Islamic State, the idea of a resolution was almost unthinkable; now a deal is conceivable, perhaps necessary for both sides. The collapse of the notion of the nation-state across northern Iraq and much of Syria, the infighting between rival movements within Sunni Islam in the region, and the key role that Iran can play in influencing Assad and combating Islamic State mean that the Arab Spring has provided Tehran with an opportunity to dramatically improve its international standing.

Post-Arab Spring Iran has to face subtle choices over how far it wants to ease its relations with the West by winding down its nuclear programme and continuing its fight against IS alongside a growing coalition of Sunni Arab nations and Western powers. Doing so could strengthen the hand of reformers and return Iran to the community of nations. But it would meet with stiff resistance from Iran's hardliners. Their doctrine of 'resistance' needs something to resist. And vested interests are not purely ideological – sanctions have served some members of the regime well, allowing for control of certain industries as well as the black market and the spectacular enrichment of clerics or their families.

Nonetheless, it is much harder for the hardliners to continue to define Iran's core mission as being the lone warrior against the West and most of the rest. That mission keeps Iran in the cold and does not risk opening the doors to economic expansion and political reform – both of which could, or would, inevitably follow an easing of sanctions and a thawing of international relations.

Rouhani has so far failed to deliver exactly what Iran's theocrats most deeply fear – an end to isolation. But neither has he failed. He has the potential, and the regional political space, to wrong-foot hardliners within Iran's body politic. The chaos in the Levant offers the possibility and the global community may need, may even welcome, Iran's return to the warmth of international partnership. Coming in from the cold will have its costs for Tehran. A regime that has been built on a cold shoulder may find a warm embrace even harder to accept.

# CIVIC COURAGE: THE CLUE
# TO TURKEY'S FUTURE?

## Alev Scott

WHERE WILL TURKEY be in fifteen years' time?
A country that is affected day to day by war-stricken
neighbours, deepening social polarisation and an
ongoing existential debate about its Islamic identity
and role in the Middle East would be a challenge for
any bookmaker or pundit. Living through the changes
has been disorientating, but in many ways the picture
in fifteen years is brighter than the events of tomorrow.

Since the start of the Arab Spring and Turkey's
accompanying reactions and experiences, I have
swung from optimism to pessimism and settled on one
hopeful truth: Turkey's political dramas may be impossible to predict but the Turks who protested against
the destruction of a park in Istanbul in the summer
of 2013 still turn up to protest about autocratic decisions and miscarriages of justice, despite the dangers
of trigger-happy and arrest-prone riot police. These
people display a bravery that holds hope for the future,
while exposing the profound problems of today. There

are reasons to trust in the potential of the younger generations, and this hope can perhaps be extended to other countries in the Middle East.

I offer a triptych of scenes to illustrate the paths open to Turkey: the first is a huge crowd in Taksim Square, Istanbul, in June 2013. It is a weekday afternoon, but the square is full of people of all ages who have left work or school to come and celebrate the survival of Gezi Park, a rare patch of greenery the government recently vowed to build over. The riot police have gone. The mood is buoyantly happy, free food and water are handed out and somewhere in the crowd people are singing: a fleeting Utopia. This is the direct result of thousands of citizens coming together to block bulldozers and police, and Gezi has come to symbolise much more than a park. This is a celebration of civic courage.

The second scene is also a protest, but the mood is very different – tense and fearful. It is 31 May 2014, the first anniversary of the initial raid on Gezi Park. Taksim Square has been closed off and guarded in advance by thousands of policemen with sub-machine guns who have learned valuable lessons in repression from last year. A small group of Gezi veterans have gathered in the streets nearby, intimidated by the masked police facing them but holding their ground. Suddenly, someone throws a bottle from a window above and it smashes in the road between the two groups. The police point their guns at the protesters, who retreat a small distance. It is a physical stand-off that mirrors the stand-off between the government and the considerable segment of Turkish society that has chosen to challenge the crackdown on dissent. Where will this stand-off end? The pessimistic answer is full-scale authoritarianism, and this is a real possibility.

The third scene is a rally in the rural town of Kocaköy in the Kurdish region of Diyarbakir, in south-east Turkey. A woman is addressing the crowds through a megaphone – 33-year-old Berivan Elif Kiliç, a mother of two and former child bride with no education, representing the pro-Kurdish Peace and Development Party (BDP). Berivan wears a headscarf and looks like she has just wandered out from the crowd herself. The nearby house where she lives is modest, like any other on that street. She is the antithesis of the typical Turkish politician accompanied by motorcade, bodyguards and ego. While some of the townsfolk dismiss her, many others – especially women – are listening closely, impressed by her ambition in the overwhelmingly male world of Turkish politics, and see her as a role model (ironically, the name of their village, 'Kocaköy', means 'husband village'). Berivan wins the municipal election a few days later (30 March 2014) and sets about encouraging the women and teenage girls in her constituency to discover their independence: to report abusive husbands, to insist on their right to continue school and to work. This is what progress looks like.

Three scenarios that signal possible directions for Turkey: a happy moment of peaceful but determined protest; an uneasy and dangerous stand-off between citizens and state; and a woman speaking to a village crowd about everyday democracy. Which will be the most dominant notes in fifteen years' time? Turkey's disputed period of democratisation has been a roller-coaster in recent years. As lately as 2010 or early 2011, the country was seen as a beacon of hope for the Middle East. Under the AKP, the Justice and Development Party that came to power in 2002 and flourished under the leadership of Recep Tayyip Erdoğan, Turkey appeared to have brought to fruition a long-awaited marriage of Islam and democracy. The apparently Western-friendly, so-called 'moderate Islamic' ruling party was achieving great things: a rapidly growing economy, more efficient public services, greater freedom of religion, intensified EU negotiations and an enviable volume of trade with both Eastern and Western partners. Turkey was the promising new power of the region.

In its heyday up to 2010, the AKP's foreign policy consisted of 'zero problems with neighbours'. Although arguably never a very realistic policy, it unravelled in the wake of the Arab Spring (along with much else in the Middle East), and most saliently through Turkey's engagement with the Syrian uprising and the subsequent years of brutal war. Before the Arab Spring, Turkey had fairly warm relations with the Syrian government. Syrian president Bashar al-Assad and Erdoğan were personal friends, but that amity quickly collapsed after Erdoğan called Assad in the early days of the unrest and attempted to advise him on how to deal with the spiralling protests.

Turkey's geographic position, especially in relation to Syria and Iraq, means it automatically has a difficult juggling act in foreign policy. However, many of its problems are self-inflicted. It has become embroiled in the Syrian war not only by proximity but through its apparently indiscriminate support of rebels, effectively giving the Syrian war a platform in Turkish territory near the borders and arguably accelerating the rise of radical Islamic groups such as ISIL. While Turkey has been, and should be, commended for its great generosity to nearly 2 million Syrian refugees so far, the free passage granted not only to refugees but to rebel fighters across the Turkish–Syrian border, at least in the early years of the war, has worsened the inevitable problems of proximity to a warzone. Jihadist recruitment in vulnerable neighbourhoods, sleeper cells, kidnappings, hostage-taking and the risk of large-scale terrorist attack by groups like ISIL have been increased, meaning that Ankara now has its hands tied in dealings with these extremist groups. Turkey's current position has in turn caused diplomatic problems with the West, as, for example, in the case of the siege of Kobane in September 2014, which I will discuss later, or the simple fact that the US has carried out remote airstrikes against ISIL without the cooperation – in fact, against the wishes – of a hugely important NATO ally.

Internally, Turkey has also undergone its own series

of challenges (including what the government calls an attempted 'coup' by followers of the America-based cleric Fetullah Gülen in late 2013). As a result, the AKP government became ever-more paranoid and suppressive when it came to public opposition in any form, so that Turkey began to look like an increasingly *undemocratic* place. The uncompromising attitude of the AKP government in recent years extended to its foreign policy, so that Turkey's relationships with regional neighbours, as well as with previously solid Western allies, have become increasingly strained, very far from 'zero problems'. The architect of that policy, Ahmet Davutoğlu, followed Erdoğan as prime minister and continued to depict Turkey as the leading light of the Middle East, in a recycled and grandiose Ottomanesque vision of regional hegemony. There are both ideological and practical problems with Turkey 'leading' a complex region in various states of civil war, not least Turkey's own problems of polarisation and authoritarianism.

How bad is the bigger picture? While Turkey's geopolitical importance means it will always remain 'on the map' in terms of diplomatic and trade relations for both East and West, it has lost significant allies in the Middle East – Egypt, Israel and Syria, for example – and it is more frequently, and openly, criticised by the EU and the US for breaches of human rights, leading to a feeling of isolation on all sides. Egypt is possibly the most dramatic example of diplomatic fall-out. Recep Tayyip Erdoğan, the president of Turkey since

August 2014 and before that the prime minister from 2003, was a very vocal supporter of Mohamed Morsi and the Muslim Brotherhood, and an unflinching critic of Morsi's overthrow and the consequent Sisi-led regime, the result of which was that the Egyptian ambassador was expelled from Turkey in 2013. Recent relations with Israel have also been turbulent, starting with the Israeli attack on the first *Mavi Marmara* Gaza flotilla in 2010, which led to the death of nine Turkish activists and the departure of the Israeli ambassador from Ankara. During the 2014 summer bombardment of Gaza, Erdoğan claimed that Israel was 'worse than Hitler' and would drown in its own blood, triggering the departure of more Israeli embassy staff from Ankara. In early 2015, Prime Minister Ahmet Davutoğlu and President Erdoğan welcomed Hamas leader Khaled Meshaal to Ankara after the latter's purported expulsion from Qatar, alarming Western powers, which regard Hamas as a terrorist organisation.

⋮ ⋮

Erdoğan's promotion of himself as a regional Muslim leader has had a significant part to play in Turkey's recent regional affairs. This self-promotion relied to a great extent on his very public condemnation of Israel, which earned him automatic respect in the Middle East from ordinary people, as well as on home ground. They appreciate him standing up for Palestinians and openly condemning Israel and America, and for his symbolic gestures of solidarity. For example, in August 2014 he appeared in the last session of parliament before the presidential elections (which, of course, he duly won) wearing a Palestinian keffiyeh. Photos of this act of solidarity with the victims of the Gaza bombardment were widely shared over the Arab world. Behind the rhetoric and photo opportunities, however, the facts on the ground don't quite match up. Israeli–Turkish trade, for example, is at an all-time high; in 2014 there was $5.6 billion worth of trade between the two countries, an increase of nearly 50 per cent from 2009. In short, you can read the headlines and look at what is ostensibly happening with Turkey and its relationships with Middle Eastern countries, but things are never quite what they seem to be on the ground.

In a world that is increasingly concerned with radical Islam, and looks at 'moderate' Islamic countries like Turkey to combat this radicalism, it is useful to examine what someone like Erdoğan has to say about this himself. In 2007 he responded to the label of 'moderate Islam' by saying: 'These descriptions are very ugly, offensive and an insult to our religion. There is no moderate or immoderate Islam. Islam is Islam and that's it.' Erdoğan's primary argument was that acts of terrorism should not be associated with Islam, because terrorism and acts of violence are 'incompatible with Islam'. Still, it is significant that a long-time leader of a country the West perceives as one of the most promising case studies for a moderate Islamic society roundly rejects the concept itself.

∶ ∶

So, Erdoğan has been a problematic Muslim leader and Turkey has lost important friends in the Middle East, in which case where is there potential for optimism? In a general election on 7 June 2015, days before this book went to print, the AKP lost their majority in parliament for the first time since 2002. This unexpected result came thanks to the performance of the leftist Peoples' Democratic Party (HDP), a party with Kurdish roots that managed to win 13 per cent of the vote by appealing to the wider Turkish electorate with a pluralistic manifesto promising decentralisation of power and greater rights for minorities, an attractive alternative to the AKP's polarising rhetoric and the static mainstream opposition. However, the result concerned many Turks who associate the party with the PKK, the separatist Kurdish militia based in the south-east of Turkey which carried out a slew of attacks in the 1990s, and on whose behalf the HDP negotiated with the AKP for a peace settlement. At this point, it is unclear what the future of the Turkish government will be after this dramatic shake-up of a thirteen-year-old hegemony, but I sincerely hope that an empowered opposition will benefit the country, especially with regards to the Kurdish issue. Already, greater regional pressure was pushing the AKP government in the direction of compromise, despite its stalled domestic peace settlement, when it was forced to cooperate with President Barzani of Iraqi Kurdistan in the fight against ISIL. Despite obvious difficulties, one of the most positive things I can imagine emerging from the mess in the Middle East at the moment is a friendship of necessity – a sort of marriage of convenience – between Kurdistan and Turkey. Kurdistan's forces have been at the forefront of the fight against ISIL, most famously helping to liberate the town of Kobane, near the Turkish-Syrian border, in early 2015, and taking oil-rich territories in Iraq. The Kurds of northern Iraq, and now of Syria, are becoming emboldened, and we can understand why. We can also see how the Turkish government might be forced to take them more seriously, especially with the HDP now holding eighty seats in the Turkish parliament.

In 2012, Erdoğan initiated a historic peace process with the Kurds, negotiating with the imprisoned leader of the PKK, Abdullah Öcalan, via representatives of the HDP's predecessor, the Peace and Democracy Party (BDP). These peace talks have now stalled, but for a while looked promising. In March 2013 a ceasefire was announced which, while technically unilateral on the PKK's side, was observed by both sides until May 2014, when the PKK allegedly attacked new military outposts being set up in south-eastern towns. A further blow was struck to the peace process in September 2014, during the siege of Kobane. Almost every Turk I spoke to at the time was extremely alarmed by the protests among the Kurdish communities, which erupted in response to the failure of the Turkish government to help the besieged Kurds. These protests killed thirty-one people, including three policemen, and shocked Turkish patriots with images of burning statues of Turkey's founding father, Mustafa Kemal Atatürk.

During the Kobane siege the underlying spectre of Kurdish–Turkish distrust was dramatically re-awoken. Western observers forgot that to most Turks the idea of supporting Kurdish fighters linked to the PKK (either with direct military support or by allowing arms flow) was unthinkable, despite the desperate situation of those trapped in Kobane, and the unifying horror of ISIL. The PKK attacks of the 1990s were fairly fresh in people's minds and general paranoia about the fighting in Syria was growing. Turks who think of the Kurds in those terms were never going to suddenly turn round and say, 'The Kurds are our friends now', and those Turks are also suspicious of peace-brokering parties such as the HDP. The AKP, in fact, took advantage of these suspicions when they courted nationalist voters in the run-up to elections in June 2015 by repeatedly warning the electorate of the HDP's terrorist links, raising concerns about any genuine, long-term commitment to the Kurdish peace process. Yet despite these tensions – and they are serious – it is not unthinkable that some kind of friendship of convenience might be forged between Turks and Iraqi Kurds in fifteen years' time, complemented by greater trust between Turks and Kurds living within Turkey.

⠿

What is the future of the political opposition in Turkey, especially in the wake of these elections results? Gezi Park is only one strand of popular protests; after June 2013 there were nationwide protests in response to the corruption scandal of December 2013, the Twitter ban of March 2014 and the horrific mine blast in Soma in May 2014. The protests after Soma in particular show the anger from workers and their families in response to perceived government negligence and corruption, a very different crowd to the largely left-wing and middle-class Gezi protesters who came to represent the face of 'protest' in Turkey in 2013. There was similar anger after blasts in the Ermenek mines in October 2014, but the protests were quashed as mercilessly as the Gezi protests were. However, the fact that they happened at all shows the seeds of dissatisfaction are spread over a larger swathe of the Turkish demographic than many people previously assumed – and this was proved by the June 2015 election results, when Turkey voted 'no' to the further consolidation of AKP power.

Turkey's political opposition cannot continue as it currently is, with outdated Kemalist and nationalist parties who generally fail to challenge the AKP. Its best hope involves giving a chance to the HDP, which aims to provide something for everyone – for example Alevis, Kurds, women and members of the LGBT community can vote for decentralisation and promoting the rights of minorities and women, instead of being condemned to settling for the long-established and sclerotic 'left' party, the Kemalist Republic People's Party (CHP), whose left credentials are dubious and not particularly representative of minorities. The people who came out and protested in Gezi in 2013, who were for the most part liberal, believe in principles that seem to have evaporated from the mainstream Turkish political agenda, principles that perhaps new, more democratic parties could enact.

In his contribution to this volume, Tamim al-Barghouti discusses the emergence of unity in the Tahrir Square protests – the fact that Egyptian women and men behaved differently towards each other in the sudden democratic euphoria that came out of those moments. I experienced the same thing during Gezi. My strongest hope for the future of Turkey is based on the democratic maturity, the pacifism and the sense of humour of the Gezi generation – and by 'generation' I mean all those young enough to make a difference in the decades to come, while remaining mindful of the stalwart pensioners who protested with as much passion as their grandchildren. The Gezi sense of humour – and its subversive potential – is still very much alive, as witnessed by the response to the political dramas of the past two years, and it is to be hoped that it will continue. To what extent this subversive humour will be punished, quashed or fed – or all three – may determine Turkey's direction.

This takes us back to the triptych at the start of this

essay, and the scenarios presented. Peaceful protest, violent suppression and organic, incremental democratisation are all elements in the future of Turkey, and it is impossible to predict which will be dominant in fifteen years' time. The economy, neighbouring wars and domestic party politics are unfathomable factors, but again I return to the constant quality I call the 'Gezi spirit', or civic courage, that is tried and tested repeatedly but never quite goes away. Whatever the government may throw at the Turkish people, this spirit remains the country's best long-term hope.

# LIVING AND WRITING IN THE MIDDLE EAST

## Fiction, Imagination and History

# LIVING AND WRITING IN KUWAIT: WHAT FICTION CAN DO

## Mai al-Nakib

WHAT IS LIFE LIKE for writers living and working in the Middle East? A straightforward question and yet one that is not at all easy to answer. Television and internet images make it seem as though the dominant feature of the region is that it is forever in a state of crisis. Needless to say, many of us have a legitimate bone to pick with media representations of the Middle East. However, if I'm honest, living in Kuwait as I do, it often does feel as though the world around me is on fire, on the brink of catastrophe or already there. The ongoing crises during the summer of 2014 in Gaza, Syria and Iraq are only the latest in the serial tragedies that have gripped our region.

The Gulf states might appear to be relatively calm by comparison – an air-conditioned bubble in the midst of hell. This is a mirage. First of all, there can be no real peace of mind for anyone with an ounce of humanity in them as long as the brutal suffering in the region continues. Even if you do not happen to have

145

bombs falling on your particular head today, you can't help but put yourself in the place of those – not so far away, not so different from yourself – who are not as lucky. And while it might be easier for Qatar, the Emirates and Saudi Arabia to allow themselves to believe it could never happen to them, it should be impossible for Kuwait to do so, given its own encounter with war and occupation in 1990–91.

Second, while perhaps not overtly in crisis, the Gulf states nonetheless thrum beneath the surface with a disparate range of problems that could erupt in the not too distant future. Reliance on a single resource is, perhaps, the most obvious concern, but other issues include demographic imbalances, fundamentalisms, sectarianisms, political disenfranchisement, environmental ruin, obesity and diabetes, masked unemployment, labour exploitation, a failing system of education and hyper-consumerism. The current state of affairs is unsustainable both materially and ethically. Gulf citizens may bury their heads in the sand but, soon enough, these issues will surface, and it doesn't take an expert to recognise that the cumulative outcome will be grave.

So, amid seemingly endless regional disasters and local difficulties, how does a writer write? With the stresses and sorrows of war, the anxiety over bleak future projections and the guilt of knowing that people nearby are experiencing intolerable suffering, how does a writer from my part of the world manage it? I can attempt a response to this question by addressing another one: what can fiction do? As a professor of English and comparative literature, this question is always on my mind as I teach students and reflect on the relevance of my research. As a writer of fiction, it is a question that informs everything I write. In brief, as far as I'm concerned, the special function of fiction is to invent worlds, to imagine alternatives to the present, to conjure up what Edward W. Said, in a different context, describes as 'eccentric angles', in order to remind us of our shared interests, if not our shared humanity.[1] Fiction can produce these effects in a myriad of inventive ways, some of which may include revisiting forgotten elements of the past; producing the conditions necessary for readers to inhabit different modes of life; and drawing attention away from a dominant order that often seems to choke off any sense of possibility. One way to convey this function of literature is through my specific experience as a Kuwaiti writer.

I was a child in Kuwait in the 1970s and came of age there in the 1980s. For me, those decades mark Kuwait's golden years. Of course, this is a view tainted by nostalgia; it is politically and historically inaccurate. In fact, those decades were marked by the Iraq–Iran War; the Souk al-Manakh stock market crash; the rise of Islamic fundamentalism; the clampdown against segments of the Kuwaiti population, the Shia community in particular; and the policy of Kuwaitisation, which threatened members of the non-Kuwaiti population, including Palestinians. Still, as a teenager growing up in the 1980s in Kuwait, I experienced some of the residual cosmopolitanism that had character-ised the country's previous history. It is this currently ignored characteristic of Kuwait that I attempt to revisit in some of the stories that appear in my book *The Hidden Light of Objects*.

Kuwait was a thriving commercial port town from the 1700s. Accustomed to travel and movement, its population – whether seafarers or Bedouin, rulers or merchants – developed canny negotiating capacities and expressed a decidedly outward-looking slant on the world. Historically, it is fair to say that Kuwait and its population have tended to be globally inter-active, managing to maintain autonomy over the centuries, walking a precarious tightrope across the Ottoman Empire, central Arabia, Britain and Iraq. I would argue that Kuwait's past successes were a result precisely of its outward-looking, engaged, generally tolerant sensibility. This particular point of view also defined the early years of Kuwait's establishment as a modern nation-state. From the 1930s onwards, up until the 1970s, Kuwait welcomed people in, tended not to see them as outsiders but, rather, as participants in the development of a shared country. We know this because in the 1950s and 1960s Kuwaiti citizenship was offered to individuals of various nationalities in a way that would never occur today.

I must insert a caveat here in order to prevent myself from slipping too far into the dangerous trap of nostalgia. Kuwaiti political scientist Abdul-Reda Assiri has argued that over time Kuwaitis developed what he calls a 'siege mentality', which emerged as a result of real threats to the state's survival.[2] For example, immediately upon declaring its political independence in 1961, Kuwait was threatened by Iraq with annexation. This threat was countered by British military protection, as well as – paradoxically – the support of 2,000 Saudi troops. I say 'paradoxically' because historically there had not been much love lost between the two nations or their leaders. From the Wahabi attacks against Kuwait from the late eighteenth to the early twentieth centuries, to the Uqair Protocol of 1922, which saw Kuwait lose two-thirds of its land to Saudi Arabia by way of the British, to crippling trade sanctions imposed by Saudi Arabia against Kuwait from 1928 to 1937, the relationship between Kuwait and Saudi Arabia has been fraught, to say the least. The vexed nature of this relationship has been overshadowed by the more recent hostilities from Iraq. Needless to say, the 1990 invasion did nothing to ease this Kuwaiti disposition. Still, Assiri suggests that, despite its defensive inclination, what kept Kuwait reasonably stable and secure over hundreds of years was the 'external outlook' of its population, shaped by the country's 'interaction with faraway lands and people'.[3]

In the 1970s, this more open sensibility still dominated my parents' generation. My parents and their contemporaries were taught mainly by Palestinian teachers at primary, secondary and university levels. Many of that generation continued their education abroad and most, if not all, then returned back to Kuwait in their prime, eager to build their country according to the exciting range of images and experiences collected along the way. Furthermore, it was a sensibility passed on to their children, those of us who grew up in the 1980s. As was evident in the streets of Salmiya or Hawalli or among the student bodies at international or even government schools, the texture of our community was decidedly varied and complex and, for the most part, it was harmonious.

After 1991, however, Kuwait's historical cosmopolitanism began to recede and its 'siege mentality' to intensify. In some ways, a more inward-looking attitude is understandable. Interactive policies and tolerance appeared to have brought nothing but catastrophe to the country and its citizens, so it was believed that something drastic and different needed to be done. Cosmopolitanism, it seemed, had been part of the nation-state's downfall, so something else needed to be slotted in its place. Expulsion, restriction and purity were chosen over inclusion, openness and plurality. In the last two decades, however, that alternative has proved to be even more catastrophic than the original crisis that initiated the shift away from cosmopolitanism. Since 1991 at the very latest (arguably even a decade before that), the relative stability enjoyed by Kuwait since the 1700s has come undone on many fronts – political, social, economic, cultural. This is not the place to enumerate all the various crises Kuwait has been through in the last two and a half decades, but a few examples would include the routine dissolutions of parliament since 2006; the disenfranchisement of the *bidoun* (those without citizenship); the escalation of tensions between the government and various opposition groups; an intensification of sectarian divisions; a worrying increase in violence; ongoing human rights concerns regarding expatriate labour as a result of the *kefala* (sponsorship) system and lack of protection; the marked decline in educational standards; an increase in health issues and the inability of the health-care system to keep up with demand; the traffic fiasco; and, above all, the predicament of dependency on a single natural resource. Something to consider is whether the absence of the cosmopolitanism that buoyed Kuwait through previous crises, excised post-1991, leaves the country ill-equipped to address the seemingly insurmountable crises suffered today.

Robert J. C. Young has argued that the *Convivencia* in Cordoba – the period of religious coexistence among Muslims, Jews and Christians in southern Spain that began under Caliph Abd-ar-Rahman III, who ruled from 912 to 961 – stands as an exemplary model of multicultural tolerance and of 'communal living in a pluralistic society'.[4] He suggests that such forms of multiculturalism continue to exist in some Gulf states even today. I would argue that historical Kuwait town and Kuwait as a young nation-state retained aspects of this key feature. *Convivencia* was sustained, Young points out, not by the erasure of difference or homogenisation in the name of nationalism or religious purity.

*Kuwait University students in the 1960s. Kuwait, by Oscar Mitri (Kuwait: Government Press, 1969), p. 17.*

On the contrary, as he explains, 'The state becomes stronger through the tolerance of heterogeneity, weaker by repressing it.'[5] Sadly, the validity of this paradox seems regionally and globally unintelligible, or perhaps just unacceptable.

This was certainly the case in 2004, when I started teaching at Kuwait University. It became abundantly clear to me that any residue of the cosmopolitan Kuwait I grew up in was not only gone, but that its memory was being systematically obliterated. This was happening at an alarming rate on many fronts: in education, in the urban landscape, in the shifting demographic, in politics, culture, clothing, language and so on. It seemed almost as if we, citizens of Kuwait, were slipping into a state of amnesia. For example, while discussing a collection of photographs of Kuwait by the well-known Egyptian photographer Oscar Mitri with my undergraduate students during that first year, I was startled to discover just how unfamiliar Mitri's Kuwait seemed to them. The book, printed by the government in 1969 and titled, simply, *Kuwait*, featured, among many other images, a religious ceremony at the Roman Catholic church, women waterskiing along the shore and a class of female university students, not one of them wearing the hijab. My students, the majority of whom were wearing the hijab, were baffled, as was I, though not for the same reasons.

This shift in outlook felt incredibly stifling to me, and one reason I turned to fiction was as a way to open a window, a vignette on to something else. My short stories attempt to revisit this forgotten or stifled cosmopolitanism in Kuwait and the wider region in an effort to imagine alternatives to the present, a different kind of home. Although my academic writing engages similar concerns, fiction possesses a flexibility and potential reach that make it particularly appealing. In any case, at the time it felt like no matter how many articles I wrote, none could match the visceral effect of fiction, my first love.

In some ways, it is impossible to escape the traces

that make us who and what we are. We are born in a particular place, into a specific family with its own distinct history. We grow up inhabiting a certain language, among a defined community of people. All these elements, among others, shape us and our perspectives on the world. For a writer, these traces pierce through the writing in one way or another. It is impossible to think of Márquez without Colombia, Rushdie without India or Mahfouz without Egypt. Nonetheless, fiction is the unique site where it is possible to escape or transform these very traces. It is true that these traces make us who we are, the kinds of writers we become. But the writing we do allows us to flee the confines of these determining factors, to imagine other worlds. For me, writing fiction became a way to recreate or reimagine a place I was convinced had once existed but that was now nowhere to be found. I needed to construct a space – a safe haven – where I could not only remember my version of the adventurous and mongrelised past, but also imagine a future other than the one that was being prepared for us by the rather rigid and extreme orthodoxies dominating the region post-9/11.

Fiction invites us to remember (or to experience for the first time) pasts that are different from the normative version of the past most expedient to current interests. If we take this function of fiction seriously, it opens up for us the chance to consider otherwise disregarded (sometimes discarded) futures. Memories, images or narratives that contradict or interrupt

*Andy Warhol exhibited his work in Kuwait
in 1976 (Sultan Gallery Archives).*

those offered up as definitive, as set in stone, remind
us that the world need not proceed as it happens to
be proceeding at present. In the context of Kuwait,
for example, what would it be like to remember that
Andy Warhol exhibited at the Sultan Gallery in 1976?
Or to remember that at the Gazelle Club, among other
venues, drinking and dancing were not the exception? Or to remember that Kuwait University was not
segregated when it was first founded and was co-ed
until 1996? Or that in 1957 the Council for Education
introduced a short dress with red ribbons as the school
uniform for girls in place of the by then contested
abaya? What would it be like to remember that, until
1991, 380,000 Palestinians lived in Kuwait, with little
inconvenience to Kuwait and much mutual benefit?

That Saudi Arabia was as much a threat to Kuwait's sovereignty as Iraq? In other words, what would it be like to remember experimentation and pushing boundaries rather than rigidity and burying our heads in the sand? At a time when so much outside the world of fiction seems to be screeching, emphatically, 'No!', it is fiction we can rely on – as I have for most of my life – to insist, stubbornly, despite everything, 'Yes!'

In addition to alerting us to alternative versions of the past, present and future, fiction also reminds us that our point of view is not the only viable point of view out there. Our life is one among billions. Other people's individual stories matter as much as our own, though in this time of socially networked self-promotion, this reality is too easily ignored. And while social networking and access to electronic data may give the impression of being hooked into difference and/or otherness, of having an immediate connection to the world at large, this immediacy may, in fact, produce the opposite effect. In 24/7, Jonathan Crary writes, 'Part of the modernized world we inhabit is the ubiquitous visibility of useless violence and the human suffering it causes. This visibility, in all its mixed forms, is a glare that ought to thoroughly disturb any complacency, that ought to preclude the restful unmindfulness of sleep.' The problem with our 24/7 access to images and information is that it does not, in fact, disturb our complacency. Never was this insight proved truer than in the summer of 2014. This is not to say that the images we view and articles we read online about individuals, nations and events, among other things, do not touch us; simply that the outcome of this scrutiny is not always (or even often) ethical practice. As Crary puts it, 'The act of witnessing and its monotony can become a mere enduring of the night, of the disaster.'[6]

In contrast to the speed of digital time, the pace of fiction is slow. Fiction produces the conditions necessary for readers to inhabit different modes of life intimately because reading is a process that takes time. The attention and focus it requires produce this intimacy between reader and text. In one way or another, we, as readers, are invested in what we read or we wouldn't do it. We come to care about the characters or the style or the place or whatever else in the book we happen to be reading. Fiction builds bridges between far-flung people and places and times in ways that might never be possible otherwise – certainly not through ever-shorter online articles, blogs, fluid newsfeeds, 140-character Tweets, Instagram images and all the many other forms of digital detritus. Fiction, with its slower-paced (intransigent?) temporality, gives us the time we need to really explore difference – lives and experiences different from our own, times and places different from our own, beliefs and values different from our own. In so doing, it produces the conditions for an ethics of otherness. By inhabiting difference through fiction – slowly, closely – I would suggest we become less likely to want to attack, colonise, oppress or homogenise the unfamiliar, whether politically, economically, socially, culturally or militarily. When we read Ghassan Kanafani's plangent short stories about Palestinian children, for example, the number of young civilian deaths in Gaza takes on an altogether different resonance. Instead of numbers and media abstractions, they become Kanafani's children, singular lives and irreplaceable futures snuffed out.

On this understanding, reading or writing fiction is no idealist escape from reality, no utopian castle in the sky. Fiction becomes a constituting factor in the production of an ethics of otherness, a global ethics we could put to work towards a more equitable common future. This may seem a heavy task to place upon the shoulders of fiction, but in my estimation fiction's shoulders are broad enough to take it. In the face of a world that seemingly shuts its ears to the lament of intolerable life, in the Middle East among other regions, fiction listens to and relays, among other things, our shared humanity.

Edward W. Said remained an unapologetic humanist to the end, albeit a refigured, post-Enlightenment humanist. For him, fiction was a humanising force whose power should not be underestimated. In *Orientalism*, he notes that Arabic literature was conspicuously absent from early Middle East Studies departments in the United States. This made it possible for experts to rely on '"facts," of which a literary text is perhaps a disturber'.[7] Literary texts disturb seemingly incontrovertible 'facts', rigidities of all sorts. Literary texts remind us of (or alert us to) alternatives to normative views and widespread perceptions. Bite-sized 'facts', digitally circulated at lightning speed, produce familiar dehumanising stereotypes, such as, 'all Arabs are terrorists' or 'all Americans are infidels'. Literature – in its regular refusal to regurgitate such 'facts' as a matter of course – interrupts these counterproductive, dehumanising axioms. Never has this particular function of fiction been more urgent in relation to the Middle East than at this moment. Never has it been more urgent in the Middle East itself than now.

# WRITING THE MIDDLE EAST, WRITING GAZA

## Selma Dabbagh

WHEN I WAS FIRST ASKED to participate in a panel entitled 'Living and Writing in the Middle East' I wondered if I was an impostor, as I don't live in the Middle East any more, although I have lived there for more than half my life. I also write in English, which presents me with a separate set of challenges and advantages from those who write in Arabic. Born in Scotland and working in London, I am a British-Palestinian writer who has lived in a scattering of Arab countries – but only for a short time in Palestine. My first novel, *Out of It*, was set in an imagined Gaza that I had only briefly visited. The tension and interaction between the real and the imagined are fertile grounds for literature, but have particular resonance in writing Palestine. After all, my experience of imagining Palestine is not that different from the experience of many Palestinians in the diaspora – as well as so many other exiles and migrants. As an outsider looking in, a woman constantly on the move with a plethora of identities, am I an impostor or a writer whose vantage point can tell us something about the dilemmas and prospects of writing about the Middle East today?

I briefly suggest that the terrain of fiction, or indeed other works of the imagination, from the Middle East, as received by Western audiences at least, has moved from sex to death: from the titillation of *One Thousand and One Nights* in the nineteenth century to an association of Middle Eastern literature with war, destruction and oppression.

Contemporary writers from the Middle East are therefore presumed to be political. Cultural expectations differ as to whether this is a positive expectation when it comes to the role of the novel. In the Western tradition, the novel is traditionally assumed to be not political, whereas in the Palestinian novel, and to a lesser extent with novels about the Arab world in general, the presumption is reversed.

When my novel started out, I wasn't quite sure where I was going to place it. I began writing it when the Gulf War erupted in 2003. I had this image of a boy on a roof and he was leaping and there was a fighter jet, but I had the idea that I would situate it in a place that was non-identifiable. Islamophobia was high at the time, and I thought that if I kept place names and the names of the characters out and had Xs and Ys instead, I could cut through a lot of prejudices about the region by explaining it as an unnamed place. I found that there was something in that idea, but I needed to bring it down to earth and locate it somewhere. I decided on Gaza because it felt to me that Gaza was the extremity of the Palestinian situation in terms of the siege by land, sea and air, and also because of the youth of the population, the number of refugees who lived there. The existence of different factions and the Palestinian leadership who had returned also brought to the fore other issues pertinent to where Palestinian society is now. So that was where I decided to place the novel.

When I started, I had this idea that I would be writing a great Palestinian novel that was an epic – it would start in 1948 or just before and it would chart the major events in Palestinian history. But it felt very heavy to me; I didn't want to go through that history again, having read many memoirs that had covered it already. I wanted to start now, and by starting now I also wanted to keep it light, and I wanted to have an energy and a youthfulness in my work. I decided to focus on the younger generations, as they captured the energy found in Palestinian society, and also because the population of Gaza, which is where I decided to base most of my novel, is so young.

I also wanted to take young people from one extremity of Palestinian society – the children of PLO exiles – and bring them back to Gaza to expose the range of Palestinian identities within the book. I wanted to explore their youth and their energy with regard to political commitment. That was my idea, and I also wanted to write about people who were so competent and had so much energy and hope but no obvious outlet for any of it.

I developed a fictional Gaza. I had a map on my desk that had 'refugee camp', 'wall' and 'café' on it, and my characters moved between these places. I researched it online, looking at blogs, by reading memoirs and talking to friends, but I researched it from the outside, so it was an impressionistic view constructed externally. I have occasionally met people who have said, 'Well, there isn't a café like that in Gaza', but that was not the point – there might be one in Ramallah, I just transposed it. I had to have that kind of a canvas for place because of the nature of my novel and where I was. It freed it from a particular time period, which also meant that I had more flexibility and fluidity in allowing the characters to move, in terms of their not having to move around fixed historical events.

It was a very strange experience going into Gaza after writing it fictionally. I had been there before, but it was odd visiting and seeing whether I'd got it right. I had a mental checklist, thinking, 'Yes, there are boys with ponytails' or, 'Yes, people do these activities' – things that you can't research. I did, however, fluctuate a lot when considering whether I had got the tonality of the place right. I would speak to one particularly bright student and feel that I had been too pessimistic, whereas another person's account would make me feel the situation was far bleaker. One Gazan journalist said I wrote about the place as though I had lived there all my life, which was, of course, deeply satisfying.

The idea that the novel should be separated from politics and that novelists have no role in politics is an old debate in the West, but the pressures on Arab novelists to be political have never been more pertinent than they are now. During the Arab Spring, fiction writers from the Middle East were brought forward to be spokespeople, taking on the role of social commentator. How much fiction writers wish to embrace this role is a very individual matter and as people who write about areas in conflict writers are constantly having to come up with tests in their mind as to where they place themselves on that spectrum; how much they want to become overtly political, what they will and will not comment on, which platforms they will or will not appear on, essentially how much they are willing to pin their colours to the mast. Many fiction writers are not natural campaigners, because they are not skilled that way, or comfortable with the role, or equipped to carry it out.

Writers may also be reluctant to turn themselves into campaigners because it may disrupt the space they need to inhabit to create and the potential of the space they wish to create. Milan Kundera described this aspect of the novel as 'the imaginary terrain where moral judgement is suspended'. Part of the idea behind the world of fiction is that you are asking people to enter a non-judgemental space and to be carried by the movement of the characters, their personal emotional experiences and the moral conflicts that they face.

A writer cannot exist without readers. English-language fiction readers, I have been led to understand by journalists and publishers, tend to veer away from the Middle East. It's all too dark, too depressing, too political. At least Latin America has sex and magic. Middle Eastern books have no wizards or bondage and there's an irrational sense that Arabs don't really ever fall in love properly. An Arab name can be an albatross around the writer's neck. It is a positive if you define yourself as an 'authentic voice', a spokesperson for the people from where your name originates, but it is unlikely that many publishers will encourage you to write a novel about adultery in Milton Keynes or a transvestite detective in Lisbon with a name like mine. Internationally these trends are starting to be challenged by writers like Michael Ondaatje, Kazuo Ishiguro and Aminatta Forna, who write successfully about characters and geographies distant from their place of origin. It is for Arab novelists writing in English to start opening up wider areas for themselves in the world of fiction, to enable greater experimentation and to challenge preconceptions, to allow for an international belief that artistic excellence is capable of stemming from this region (these names), not just in depicting the region but by analysing more broadly, in a stylistically innovative way, the human condition.

By contrast, Arab novelists writing in Arabic and based in the Arab world can often develop strong localised followings. Their writing captures the nuance, dialectic variation and humour of specific locales. They can capture the spirit of the time and enrich their work with contemporary references. Their writing has a significant local or regional readership. These writers occupy a terrain off bounds to most Arab-origin writers who write in other languages or live outside the Arab world. There is neither the proximity nor the voice.

These Arab-language, Arab-world writers are, however, not supported in the way writers are supported in the West and face additional obstacles when aspiring to reach a broader audience. There are few grants and little state investment in the profession. The film industry in Morocco, Jordan, Lebanon and Syria has had more success than the impoverished quaint band of writers of novels and short stories, who still very much go it alone. State censorship on matters sexual and political can demand a level of inventiveness that few Western writers have to even contemplate. Distribution channels in the Arab world are shoddy, copyright protection is weak, agents rarely exist, the idea of books being edited is a curious one. On top of this there is war, occupation, social and political uncertainty and economic austerity in many areas. If I compare myself with the students I met when I was in Gaza, I do not have to deal with electricity outages because the local power station has been bombed; I do not have to read at night by candlelight unless I am feeling particularly whimsical.

If, after this huge struggle, an Arab writer manages to get his or her work to a significant readership the chances of its becoming an international work are small. The book will need to surmount the barriers of translation and publication, as well as the *Who's this Muhammad? Where's the wizard?* prejudices of the book buyer before it has any chance of being a success in the international market. And even then, if the writer succeeds, there's no guarantee that things will go smoothly. Take Khaled al-Khamissi, who wrote the exceptional *Taxi* (2006), a work that documented with humour, imagination and wit the trials and tribulations of Cairo's population at cracking point by depicting the immense potential and everyday heroism of Cairenes, even though he was invited to the Edinburgh International Book Festival, he was denied a visa to enter the UK.

I am always aware of my advantages.

Ahdaf Soueif is eloquent in articulating the idea that there are few people who inhabit the middle ground between the East and the West, and as an British-Palestinian English-language writer I place myself firmly in that *mezzaterra*. I am aware that there is a body of opinion that gained ground during the anti-colonial struggles of the last century that rails against the writing of the histories of formerly colonised people by people of the previously colonising nations. There was a resistance to histories being 'appropriated'. Writers were encouraged to stay close to their country's dialects and language and to 'decolonise the mind' of the language of the empire. The battle on this front has not ended, but as someone from a coloniser–colonised heritage in a globalised world, I am representative of how complicated a formulaic application of tests as to who can write what, and how, is likely to become.

My own tests have focused more on content than on form, on authors' levels of sensitivity towards their subject matter and their responsibility towards it. I concentrate on the way a writer writes rather than on who the writer is in terms of national origin.

There are several difficulties with writing about Palestine. I heard an Israeli academic say that, if you are going to write about this region, there is nothing you can do, because whatever you do you are going to get it in the neck, which I thought was a rather fine way of putting it. However, I have since learned from writer friends that writing about Gaza is nothing compared to the troll activity that will set itself upon authors who write about Virginia Woolf or William Shakespeare. When I first started writing, I had an expectation that I would come up against the Zionist lobby very strongly. That was one concern. The other concern was about not being true or honest, or being somehow irresponsible with the subject matter I was dealing with. I was far more concerned about my Palestinian readership and they have been, in the main, extremely supportive. I was humbled by how much it meant to people in Gaza that I had tried to ensure their troubled land's place on the literary map.

I have had some negative feedback, which is to be expected: people's beliefs get rattled, they feel threatened. These were mainly knee-jerk reactions of an ill-informed, rather stupid variety. Who you are, where you stand and how you deal with your subject matter are important, and they affect style.

Another aspect of writing novels about this part of the world is that people have this anticipation of dullness. They feel that they have to go into it with a heavy heart; they would perhaps rather have their teeth pulled than read about Palestine and Israel. The writer needs to inject energy, colour and life, to bring in an emotional story that resonates. I had always wanted to be a writer, but in my mid-twenties I read a book (*The Long Night of White Chickens* by Francisco Goldman) that was an amazing love story set in Guatemala, and after that I became obsessed with Guatemala – I took to scanning the papers for stories about Guatemala, when I had known nothing of the place before I read the novel.

I've developed some personal views with regard to what role literature has in our highly politicised environment, and I'll list them now.

One is quite obvious: to bear witness and to reclaim history. We are forgetting our own histories. I've met Palestinian journalists who grew up in Jordan and didn't know that Palestinians were expelled from Kuwait in 1990 and 1991. This is the challenge of reclaiming the very recent past, in a way that brings it to life.

Another is to help visualise the future: to find ways of encouraging hope, strength and endurance. A project called 'Decolonizing Architecture' made this point very strongly to me. The architects proposed ways of converting installations serving the

Israeli military occupation to places for the occupied population. How the walls around settlements would come down, how watchtowers could be converted into bird sanctuaries, how skate parks could replace checkpoints. At first I thought this was nonsense; it was never going to happen, so what were the funders thinking? But my initial rejection was precisely the reason why I ultimately embraced it. I realised how mentally blocked I was at seeing beyond the current impasse and how much of what I read and mulled over focused on problems and not future solutions.

The trouble with translating such positive thinking into literature is that you can easily move towards writing that has a whiff of propaganda about it. Margaret Atwood has a warning for writers: 'Beware the leitmotif.' My warning is: 'Beware the message.' It's very difficult for works of fiction to sustain heavy messages, for the reason that I mentioned before – the need for lightness and a belief by the readership that they're entering a world where they're being led by characters, not by an outside force that's driving them one way or the other. Less is sometimes more in terms of presenting political realities in fiction.

Another role of the writer is to create the 'psychiatric notes' of a society – to see all elements of one's society from the most marginalised to the most central within it, to create an awareness of who we, as a people, have become, how we treat each other, how our behaviour impacts upon others.

A writer can also provide solace or comfort through

an expression of a commonly shared experience. It was extremely satisfying for me to have Palestinian friends read my book and say to me, 'I knew exactly who that character was. It was Aboud. It was Foulan.' It wasn't Aboud or Foulan, I didn't know anyone with those names, but they could feel that they knew the characters so well. It's about not feeling so alone. But it is also very important to me that literature challenges and interrogates society. It's not just about making people feel comfortable about the way things are, because the situation has never been worse. It's about how we can change things that are under our control, even if the most critical aspects of our life are not under our control at all (as in the case of Gaza).

The last challenge is actually quite controversial, although it doesn't sound it. It's the idea of creating beauty. What is the space for creating beauty in literature and other work when you're under situations of such extreme strife? There's a poem by Pablo Neruda that says in effect, 'How can I write about flowers and volcanoes when there's the blood of children in the streets?' But in the Palestinian situation, when such a protracted, brutal set of circumstances is being faced by generation after generation, one starts to think of the role of the artist as being someone who creates something that you're fighting for and not just someone who expresses what you're fighting against – someone to portray what is already good, heroic and in many cases absurdly funny about your current reality.

As a writer, you're never sure when you write on

Palestine whether you have any value as a craftsperson. If somebody praises your work you think, 'Well, you're only praising it because you like my politics', and if they hate it you think, 'You're only hating it ...' You never feel that you're really being viewed as a person with a skill who made innumerable decisions to arrive at that particular piece of work. When I occasionally meet someone who says, 'I thought that opening section was a bit like Dylan Thomas', or something along those lines, I get very excited.

Palestinian writers are also learning to accept the unacceptable, that their writing will sometimes just get blocked, or censored in incomprehensible ways. To dwell too much on this can turn you into a conspiracy theorist, but it does happen. Judgements have to be taken as to which battles to fight. In the meantime, you just need to try harder the next time, to be strategic, to hope the stars are configured differently, to trust that you have readers who value your work. And to remember that it is easier now than it was in the past and that we will open the way for others. *Try again, fail again, fail better*, as the Samuel Beckett postcard above my desk advises me.

There's one more specific issue and that concerns hybridity. I believe it can strengthen a writer's vision to be always a little bit outside the subject they are covering, to have an insider/outsider viewpoint and to be are aware of different cultures. Michael Ondaatje has talked about the growth of 'mongrel literature'. I like this expression. More and more of us are becoming mongrelised. There's more and more intermarriage and greater movements of people across borders. There's a global awareness, a growing cosmopolitanism, that allows for a greater understanding and more of a global identity, free of ethnic, religious and racial suspicions. I subscribe to that. I write for that.

# FICTION'S HISTORIES: WRITERS AND READERS IN THE MIDDLE EAST

**Marilyn Booth**

STANDING IN Muhammad Mahmoud Street, near Cairo's Tahrir Square, one year after the toppling of President Hosni Mubarak, I watched political banners waving in the light breeze. Satirical puppets of old-regime personalities were greeted with amusement by passers-by. Commemorative T-shirt hawkers, school-children, soapbox orators and their audiences, police vans and bicycles, all sought their place, not only at Tahrir but throughout the downtown. As I wandered around before settling down in the library for my research on nineteenth-century Egyptian literature, I absorbed a kaleidoscope of images.

Along one side of Muhammad Mahmoud Street, just off the square, the high outside wall of the American University in Cairo's old campus had become a vivid, ever-changing, visual palimpsest, an emotionally charged commentary on the Egyptian people's resistance to authoritarianism over months – and years – of speaking truth to power with their bodies and voices.

Artists young and old painted and scratched their visions on to the rough wall in a twenty-first-century equivalent to the eloquence of ancient rock paintings. Likenesses of the young martyrs of the revolution, with birth and death dates and loving tributes, seemed startling rebirths of the beautifully vital Coptic death-mask images of many centuries ago.

Another form of artistic tribute was a contemporary rendering of iconic figures from Egypt's pharaonic eras, so widely familiar from tomb paintings and temple carvings. Revolution-inspired artists painted Egyptian goddesses and pharaohs to challenge imperial authoritarian rule. 'Pharaoh' as an image of political power has a very long artistic history in Egypt. If it's an image that sparks pride, it can also gesture to ethically bankrupt authoritarian rule. One hundred and more years ago, Egyptian poets embraced the image to attack and to satirise the pretences and the very presence of British imperialist officials with their rhetoric of 'benign' colonial tutelage. The image has powerful critical purchase partly because 'pharaoh' appears in the Qur'an as an image of cruel and arrogant worldly power.

But it was the images of the ancient Egyptian goddess Nout that transfixed me. Nout is the life-giver who births the sun every morning and takes it once again into her body in the evening for safekeeping. She appears in many a pharaoh's or high official's tomb, watching over the mummy that was meant to repose there for ever. Today, Egypt's artists take icons that in ancient times supported a regime of top-down power, such as Nout, and transform them into symbols for vernacular democratic practices: Nout's sun shines down on all. A mythic history of the nation was recreated to make a new narrative, as Egyptians were striving to produce a new, just, ethically strong form of governance, not only through the state but also in institutions of social and civic life and the family, a revolutionary vision that will demand years of hard work to realise.

Throughout most of my thirty years' acquaintance with Egypt (as a student, a researcher and a some-time resident) I could have only imagined such sights occurring in fiction. This can't be happening here! But what I term 'fiction's histories' offer another insight: much of the fiction produced in Arabic over the past century suggests convincingly how ready Egyptians, and others, were for what seemed in 2011 to promise a systemic upheaval.

Indeed, the art that had taken over walls throughout central Cairo has much in common with Arabic fiction, today and in the past. Challenging 'top-down' history-writing is as central to literature as it is to visual art, post-2011 but also long before. Our series of conversations at the Edinburgh International Book Festival sought to think through the attempted unmaking or 'unravelling' of a century-old order in the Middle East. As much as we see the signs of that on the walls of Cairo, we must also remember the persistence of seemingly intractable, yet never completely impervious, obstacles to people's freedom to make themselves. That's evident in Arabic fiction from the 1890s to our own time. There seems no guarantee that a 'new order' (for better or for worse) is on the way. But fiction, in the company of the other arts, offers pathways to interrogate the persistence of old orders (such as patriarchal thinking and authoritarian structures). Reading today's fiction against the backdrop of Arabic novels written a hundred years ago is one of many ways to enrich our field of vision.

It seems no accident that in recent years the historical novel has featured prominently among Arabic fiction titles, just as it did in the late nineteenth century, early in the Arabic novel's history. Revisiting major political events or tracing a family's or a community's more intimate paths, which might intersect with or depart from the official historical narratives of the nation, historical fiction (like recreations of ancient Egyptian myth-figures) can pose a critical, alternative history of communities. It can ask, or redefine, who the subjects of history are or should be: perhaps they're not 'national subjects' but something else, or both. Selma Dabbagh's fictional Gaza, the setting for her novel *Out of It* (2011), is about a place and a community and its history or histories. It's also about diaspora as loss and community both, a situation that hovers over all Palestinian histories, as the nicely ambiguous meaning of Dabbagh's title suggests.

What is a fiction writer's responsibility to history? And how does she come to inhabit the spaces – physical, mental, imaginary – that allow her to respond to the ways history may be suppressed or narrowed or misrepresented by politicians or media discourse with historical narratives of her own making, based on imagining other lives?

Preparing for and then chairing the session at the Edinburgh International Book Festival on 'Living and Writing in the Middle East', I was struck by how the discussion we had – Mai al-Nakib, Selma Dabbagh, myself and our audience – kept on returning to history, or histories. In different ways, Mai and Selma both talked about losing the 'historical cosmopolitanism' (in Mai's words) of their nations' pasts, and how memory and collective narratives of earlier times may be lost in agendas for the present.

Now as always, at a time of ongoing crisis, retrieving – and rethinking – the narratives of history and myth, as conflictual or fanciful as these narratives may be, could be persuasive political acts. They could encourage readers to think about a future that honours *many* voices from the past. Dabbagh highlights fiction's ability to reanimate these narratives. A character in *Out of It* finds his meaning as a political person in rewriting the archival and oral histories of Palestine: history is a character who insists on answers. Al-Nakib's stories write history partly through objects we take with us when we go places, the meanings those objects have for us, the personal histories of connection and alienation they evoke.

As a translator and scholar, I have been so drawn to novels that are historical, not always in obvious ways.

Sometimes history is front and centre, as, for example, in the great activist, scholar and writer Latifa al-Zayyat's classic novel of coming-of-age feminism, *The Open Door* (1960), set in an earlier revolutionary period, the 1940s–50s, in Egypt's national history.[1] But national revolution is also – as al-Zayyat's young characters insist – about revolution in the family, about young women's and young men's right to choose their futures. The theme wasn't new in 1952, or in novels by women, but it was a liberatory moment that was celebrated, tested and criticised in fiction.

At other times history can creep in at the edges. Even when they aren't 'historical novels' in the classic sense, novels (and short stories) in the Arab world today (and in diaspora, and whether written in Arabic or in many other languages Arabs speak) are grappling with questions of history. A novel I translated recently from the Arabic, Lebanese author Hassan Daoud's *The Penguin's Song*, traces displacements that Beirut's downtown populace suffered during Lebanon's civil war (1975–90) and in its inconclusive aftermath.[2] In an isolated block of flats overlooking the old downtown, where he lived as a boy, the young-adult narrator returns obsessively to his dark shelf of old books that now mostly gather dust. Receptacles of the past, those books are where imagined lives reside, and he wonders, a bit wistfully, whether reading the same old texts could give a reader new meanings. (He thinks they can, but he doesn't open them much.) This young, disabled man brings paltry income home to his parents from proofreading, but we never learn the content of the pages he peruses for a scruffy, stingy little publishing operation stuffed into the stifling top floor of a crowded high-rise in the rebuilt city. These pages might as well be blank. They hold none of the promise of the old volumes that he cherishes (even if he rarely rereads them). *The Penguin's Song* invites readers to think about how states and political elites, as they banish people to the social and physical margins of their society, and dispossess them, destroying the old urban landscape to rebuild it for their own commercial interests, also destroy community histories. They leave young people culturally rootless, when they are already, and perhaps more than ever in recent times, socially and economically vulnerable.

How and why novelists rewrite history is a question that's led me to dwell not only in novels on the past but in the past of novels. As a scholar drawn to the Arab nineteenth century and a translator who lives, reads and translates in and of the twenty-first century, I'm struck by the continuities in themes, as well as the differences in the ways those themes are enacted in fiction. In the decades before the First World War, the Arabic novel was a new genre drawing vigorously on popular Arabic oral storytelling and its written manifestations, and equally though controversially on European traditions of realism, romance and the Gothic. It emerged and became popular in another long moment of political crisis and possibility, when well-educated reformists, some of whom (the men!) had studied in

Europe, were simultaneously excited and critical about what they saw there. In both historical novels and fictions set in their own time and place, writers took up issues of personal political liberation and freedom of choice under the many and particular stresses of the time. There was political domination under European 'tutelage', financial hardship as the Middle East was drawn more intensively into a European- and North American-centred capitalist economy, and social stress as new ways of thinking about personal – individual, family – life clashed with a firmly ensconced patriarchal family structure. Increasing educational opportunity (for some) meant that young people were asking questions in the 1890s as they do now. Arab women and men wrote fiction that explored tensions between self-making and the expectations or strictures that young women and men faced (and how those expectations differed according to whether one was female or male). Some fictions made explicit links between political tyranny and an implacable patriarchal 'right' to determine young people's futures. Novels by women highlighted the psychic, physical and social costs to young women of coerced marriage (also a theme in novels by men). The young woman who could read and write was the heroine who could – though not always – prevail. Given persistent stereotypes of Arab women – which like all stereotypes have a toehold in reality but are never all, or even most, of the reality – it may come as a surprise to readers now that turn-of-the-twentieth-century Arab women were publishing novels (and advancing decidedly feminist ideas). They were. Fictions like Zaynab Fawwaz's *Good Consequences, or the Radiant Maiden of al-Zahira* (1899),[3] Labiba Hashim's *Man's Heart* (1904), Adele Jaridini's *The Young Eastern Woman* (1909) or Afifa Karam's *Fatima the Bedouin* (c. 1910)[4] highlighted for Arabic-reading audiences the resourcefulness, outspokenness, professional aspirations and personal desires of young (and not always elite) Arab women. Some were fiercely didactic conduct-novels, earnest attempts to shape the behaviour and the expectations of young readers.

Like elsewhere in the world a vociferous debate in the Arab press over the possibly 'dangerous' impact of novel-reading on the impressionable young – particularly the female young – accompanied the exuberant production of novels (many of them adaptations from French or English works). It's true that the young heroines in these novels read – and wrote – love letters, and so maybe the parents of young readers did have reasons to worry about fiction's influence! Perhaps the more disturbing insight was that romance was political. It was all about the many levels of liberation that individuals would seek and fight for. Good governance, these novels suggest, required respectful family relations, traced especially between parents and daughters, and husbands and wives. Zaynab Fawwaz's *Good Consequences* plotted a political succession struggle, casting it as contingent on a young woman's personal struggle to be allowed to choose her (marital) future. Fari'a and Shakib fall in love over an intellectual and poetic conversation; his respect for Fari'a's choices validates his legitimacy as a future ruler. His rival is portrayed as an unacceptable ruler because of his lack of respect for Fari'a – he has his thugs abduct her repeatedly. Published in 1899, the novel reworked 1850s–1860s south Lebanese history in a way that insisted on a different historical narrative, one that brought women's and other marginalised subjects' voices into decisions on who would rule the community. The concerns are not so dissimilar to those that animated young activists in 2011 and since.

I raise this historical example because I think it is worth keeping in mind how persistent some issues are, and how youthful energies (found in humans of all ages!) continue to confront these issues. Today's literary, artistic and political activists operate in different circumstances, but the nineteenth century (like Nout) is always with us, wherever in the world we live. With all the differences acknowledged, the conflicts, stresses and inequalities that marked the world then still mark it today. It is as well also to remember the horizontal similarities across different societies – to not exceptionalise, while always remaining deeply aware of the inequalities wrought and deepened by imperialism and settler colonialism. In the 1890s, young readers in Mansura, Egypt, were immersed in romance plots little different from those capturing young readers in Manchester in England, or Lyons in France, or Hyderabad in imperial-era India. Challenges to patriarchal governance systems in family and society are not as far apart as we tend to assume. (Reading women in Egypt were well aware of suffragists' activism in Britain, and some supported them.) As today, 'globalisation' then had its liberatory and its repressive facets, and its uneven effects on class-differentiated and geographically dispersed populations.

In Afifa Karam's *Fatima the Bedouin* – a novel published in the twentieth century's first decade in Arabic in New York City – the eponymous heroine, an emigrant originally from a semi-nomadic Sunni Muslim tribe in the Lebanon, is abandoned by her lover, an elite urbanite of a Christian sect who deceived her into believing they were married before fleeing Lebanon and his parents' wrath. With her baby in her arms, wandering dazed along Broadway (yes, Broadway, where the novel begins), Fatima is accosted as a vagrant by an officer of the NYPD. She is rescued by Alice, a wealthy New York socialite and charity patron, who – we learn through their conversations – has known parallel sufferings, though within her privileged life. This fictional encounter sounds (and is) improbable, but it's a reminder that imagined lives in the past also helped writers and readers make sense of a world of bewildering journeys, aspirations dashed by oppressive mental and material structures, and, in spite of it all, affirming solidarities – the 'ethics of otherness' that al-Nakib sees as central to her own writing. Practices and desires that fiction writers scripted then, in part by writing fictional histories of their own 'earlier times', are ones we still grapple with now. Young people in Gaza, Kuwait and Lebanon – as well as New York, Mumbai and so many other places – experience them, engrave them on walls and read and write them in novels.

∷ ∷

Burdened by histories that leave them few choices, histories their elders but not they themselves have helped to shape, fictional youth in Selma and Mai's writing could, given other circumstances, be in the maidans of Cairo, Hong Kong, Bahrain, Istanbul, New York.

Of course places are not interchangeable, and fiction's capacity to evoke the *particular* geographical and built layers of community experience can help to sustain survival through archiving, or recreating, memory: Palestine and Syria today are powerful examples. The fragrance of a bulldozed orchard, the cracks in those front steps that used to be ours, that conversation the night before your brother was dragged to prison, the ball game in the street ... all the everyday lives that people everywhere work so hard to maintain and sometimes to overcome are the stuff of fiction. With the destruction of societies (some built with great suffering and dedication on the debris of earlier wars), the recording, evoking, constructing, of memories, of imagined and recalled oral histories, of that specific café on the corner and the precise taste of Grandma's soup, become part of political responsibility – the bearing of witness that our writers are so conscious of doing.

Selma built her 'fictional Gaza' – her sense of (this) place – from the memories of others, the archives of the internet, conversations and her own emplace-ments elsewhere – *that* café, but somewhere else. Selma's Gaza raises the compelling if unanswerable question of who the outsider or the insider is. Mai's Kuwait, which she feels has been 'rewritten' by new representations that she does not recognise from her childhood – a monochromatic narrative, as she sees it, of a more polychromatic, cosmopolitan place – leads us to wonder what is 'outside' or 'inside'. Time itself might make us outsiders in or to places where we think we still dwell. At the same time, the capacity we have, in our technology-driven era, to peer inside so many windows may mean more apparent access, but with it comes more responsibility: to listen, and observe, and read, humbly and widely, always conscious of our own places, the spaces – mental, physical, linguistic, political – in which we think and speak as learners, translators, writers.

The revolutionary imaginary that has emerged in so many parts of the world may be ephemeral in terms of concrete accomplishments, but it has brought youth to the forefront, a symbol of change to be sure, but also transformation's motor. That so many new writers are engaging in today's Arabic literary scene (including its blogosphere) is also a sign of this. Yet as we celebrate youthful energy, we must remember that so very many young people in the world do not have the means to be part of a motor of change, even when they have grown up in relatively comfortable circumstances. Even more when they have not: malnutrition, lack of educational opportunity or pressure to stay away from school, war as daily reality and various kinds and remnants of political violence and colonial rule, disease, sexual violence and domestic abuse – these are the unconscionable inequalities of the global system in a time when human inventiveness has more scope than ever to think of solutions. These, too, are the conditions necessary for liberatory thinking and art, along with the irrepressible affective energies of adolescents everywhere. Writing fiction, writing history, Arab authors keep readers mindful of persistent patterns but also alert us to their unravelling. And they remind us that it doesn't have to be this way.

# SYRIA IN CRISIS

# WHAT YOU DON'T READ ABOUT THE SYRIAN HUMANITARIAN CRISIS

## Dawn Chatty

IN 2012, a year into the Syrian crisis, policy pundits in the US and Europe began asking, 'Is this the end of Sykes–Picot?' In other words, is a hundred-year-old secret agreement between France and Britain that shaped the contemporary state order of the Middle East – as delineated by James Barr in this volume – coming to an end? That very question was addressed in 2014 by Abu Bakr al-Baghdadi after he declared himself the 'Caliph' – chief civil and religious ruler – of the entity known as ISIL (the Islamic State of Iraq and the Levant). His goal, he said, was to erase the borders of the modern nation-states of Syria and Iraq – and thus erase 'Sykes–Picot', which established these boundaries. But the artificiality of these borders established by the British and the French are only part of the story. The post-First World War carve-up of the region cut across multi-ethnic communities and regularly ignored natural and social frontiers. Recognising the continuities of social communities despite this carve-up can help us to make sense of the contemporary forced migration of millions of people from Syria, both within the country and across nation-state borders into Turkey, Lebanon and Jordan. With or without the Sykes–Picot borders, I will argue in this essay that many of Syria's numerous multi-ethnic, religious and tribal communities are responding to the crisis with integrity, internal social cohesion and a unified defence, even if only at the local level. While I am not contesting the powerful effects of armed conflict between state and non-state actors, I will focus on Syria's untold stories of community cohesion – and how the once marginalised, particularly the Kurds and mobile tribes, are taking on major and important roles.

Nearly 50 per cent of Syria's population has now been displaced. The UN agency for refugees (UNHCR) released figures in January 2015 confirming that more than 9 million of Syria's 22 million people have been dispossessed and displaced. Of these, 3.7 million have crossed state borders seeking refuge and asylum. We know that more than 1.1 million have crossed into Lebanon, a small country with a population of only 4.4 million. Another 1.6 million have crossed into Turkey, which has a population of over 76 million. And at least 620,000 have sought refuge in Jordan among its population of less than 6.4 million. Why have some sought refuge across national borders and others remained in Syria even when fighting has destroyed their homes and neighbourhoods? Why have some chosen Turkey, others Lebanon and still others Jordan for asylum?

Why have some who fled returned? And finally why have so few of Syria's Christian minorities fled (current figures show that they are leaving at the same rate as Muslim Sunni and ethnic-minority groups)? In other words, why has there been no mass exit of Christians or other minority groups of the sort that occurred in Iraq post-2003 (for example, Assyrian Christians and Mandeans), just the steady exits of people in family groups seeking safety and security from sites of armed conflict?

Understanding these movements means taking a bird's-eye view of the ethnic composition of both late Ottoman Syria and the modern state carved out of the general Ottoman region known as Bilad al-Sham (the Levant). Bilad al-Sham in the late nineteenth century was a region of surprising ethnic and religious complexity. In large measure as an outcome of the nineteenth-century Ottoman reforms (Tanzimat), the separate ethno-religious communities of the Levant such as the Greek Orthodox, the Nestorian Christians, the Assyrians, the Catholics, the Apostolic Armenians and the Jews engaged in officially sanctioned self-government through the *millet* system.[1] Further adding to this mix of peoples were the nearly 4 million forced migrants, largely Muslim, from the borders of the Ottoman–Russian–Austro-Hungarian empires who were dispossessed and made to leave their lands looking for sanctuary first in the Balkan provinces of the Ottoman Empire, starting from the 1860s, and later in eastern Anatolia and the Levant itself. These included Tartars, Abkhazis, Circassians, Chechnyans and Dagestani. In eastern Anatolia this influx of Muslim forced migrants resulted in tensions and localised massacres that saw Armenians and other Christian minority groups seeking asylum in Syria.

Under the mandates granted by the League of Nations – conforming to a great extent to the divisions under the Sykes–Picot Agreement – Greater Syria was divided between Britain and France. The British controlled Palestine and almost immediately subdivided it into Transjordan and Palestine. The French received – but also had to fight off deep local resistance – much of the rest of Syria, creating ever more territorial divisions: Greater Lebanon and an Alawite state along the northern Mediterranean coast, a Druze state just north of Transjordan, a Bedouin 'state' in the semi-arid desert (*badia*) of Syria and two statelets composed of Aleppo and Damascus and their hinterlands. These divisions were deeply unpopular and opposed by those nationals who felt they belonged to Bilad al-Sham. After years of revolt the French had to formally reunite the Syrian people under their mandate into one nation-state in 1936.

This same period, however, saw the acceptance of significant groups of Christian minorities from Iraq when Britain gave up its mandate over the country. The Assyrian Christians, who had served in the British Mandate Iraqi gendarmerie, felt abandoned upon the withdrawal of Great Britain in 1932 and many fled to Syria, as well as further shores. The Armenians, the survivors of the massacres and death marches of 1915 from eastern Anatolia down the Euphrates River, were also welcomed and given Syrian citizenship. Kurds fleeing the failed uprising in Turkey to restore the Islamic Caliphate (the Sheikh Said Revolt) were accepted too and given citizenship, as were the earlier wave of Palestinians entering Syria at the beginning of the Palestinian rebellion against British rule of 1936–9. These diverse groups of refugees made the modern Syrian nation-state an eclectic mix of peoples, religions and ethnicities.

Some modern historians have credited the new Syrian nation-state of 1943 as largely defined by its people's openness to accept refugees and exiles from both the post-First World War era and the inter-war mandate-period social upheavals of the Palestinians and Kurds, for example. Thus Syria, defined by its refuge-granting policy, become the epitome of multi-cultural ethnic tolerance, with Christians, Muslims, Jews and Druze living side by side among Albanians, Palestinians, Armenians, Circassians, Kosovars and Cretans, to name but a few. The fact that twice the number of Syrians displaced by fighting today have not crossed international borders in their search for safety and security but remained in the country (6 million of about 9 million) suggests that return, once the armed conflict ends, is more likely than not. What the Sykes–Picot Agreement most undermined was the cultural and social integrity of the desert-dwelling mobile tribes of Greater Syria and the Kurdish people of eastern

Anatolia. The distinction between Bilad al-Sham (Greater Syria) and the distinctive cultures of Mesopotamia (contemporary Iraq), as embodied in Basra and Baghdad and their rural hinterland, was never compromised, partially because they were mandated to two separate European powers and continued to have strong roots in pre-First World War affiliations and cultures. The border between French-mandated Syria and British-mandated Iraq followed a cultural and social frontier which had existed for centuries. In a very long view, it mirrored the differentiation between the Umayyad Caliphate, based in Damascus in the seventh and eighth centuries, and the Abbasid Caliphate, based in Baghdad from the eighth to the thirteenth centuries.

The most significant damage to the social fabric of Greater Syria was caused by the attempt to impose lines in the sand as modern borders. These, first, bisected the traditional migration routes and grazing lands of the mobile tribes of northern Arabia, cutting them off from their places of origin in the Nejd (central Saudi Arabia today) and separating them from the Syrian *badia* they had moved into in the eighteenth and nineteenth centuries. With an arm of Jordan and Iraq (the line in the sand protecting the Haifa oil pipeline drawn by Sir Mark Sykes) transecting their traditional lands, it was only a matter of time before their movements would become circumscribed and their ability to act and their powerful attachment to the Saudi Kingdom be sorely tested. For the Kurds, these lines on a map turned them into dispossessed and displaced people, even without moving. The Kurdish nation was denied a state at the Treaty of Lausanne (so, too, the Armenians), and instead helplessly saw itself divided up and made part of four new modern nation-states: Turkey, Iran, Iraq and Syria. Never before had a nation in modern history been so blatantly dissected, and this in the era of self-determination of peoples. In the post-First World War settlement, the nations of central Europe were permitted nation-statehood – for example, Czechoslovakia (1918), Austria (1919) and Hungary (1920) – but not the Kurds nor the Armenians. And of course Palestine was to be granted a British-mandated statehood, but only as long as a Jewish national home could be incubated in its core.

At least at the close of the First World War, the US president, Woodrow Wilson, expected more. In January 1919 he set out his famous 'Fourteen Points'. In a nutshell they were that there should be no more secret agreements, the League of Nations (the precursor to the United Nations) was to be established, and 'self-determination' was to be the basic principle regarding questions of sovereignty in international law. To make his points a reality, he set up the Inter-Allied Commission on Mandates in Turkey (concerning the disposition of non-Turkish areas of the Ottoman Empire). He appointed Henry Churchill King and Charles Crane to survey local opinion regarding their future. The Commission was ignored by the French and the British, who refused to send members to take part in the exercise. The Commission began its work in June 1919 and by 31 August 1919 had interviewed over 3,000 Syrians from all walks of life, including Ismaelis, Alawites, Druze, Muslims, Christians and Bedouin tribal leaders. The overwhelming conclusion was that Syrians did not wish to be divided into a northern and southern Syria. They wanted a decentralised, secular government, as was already in place under King Faisal, the son of Sharif Hussein of Mecca. They were ready to accept a League of Nations Mandate as long as it was awarded to America, or in second place to Great Britain. But under no circumstances would they accept a French mandate. By the time the report was prepared, the 1919 Paris Peace Conference had largely determined the area's future. The findings of the King–Crane Commission were in absolute contradiction to the three secret agreements (the Hussein–McMahon Accords of 1916, granting the Arabs a nation of their own; the Sykes–Picot Agreement of 1916, dividing the same region among Britain, France and Russia; and the Balfour Declaration of 1917, permitting the crea-tion of a Jewish homeland in Palestine for the Jewish people) examined by Avi Shlaim in this volume. The report was issued at the end of the summer of 1919, but it was suppressed and withheld from public dissem-ination for three years and then only released once the basic elements of the Sykes–Picot Agreement and the Balfour Declaration had been incorporated in the Covenant of the League of Nations.

In the decades that followed, both the tribes of the

Syrian desert – the Bedouin – as well as the Kurdish people – also tribal – continued to maintain their cultural integrity, despite modern borders and artificial frontiers. Syria's northern border with Iraq and Turkey was a land of Kurds who were able to move back and forth across mountainous border terrain difficult to monitor. Over time, as Kurds in these border regions opposed Turkish policy, they increasingly took refuge in Syria or in Iraq. They established and maintained social and political ties across borders and were often able to establish links that gave them, even if unofficial, laissez-passers across the Syrian–Turkish, Syrian–Iraqi and Iranian–Turkish borders superimposed over their rugged homeland.

The Bedouin of Syria once largely inhabited the Syrian *badia*, raising herds of camel, sheep and goat. They are social groups based on kinship – segmentary lineages with membership maintained by behaviour appropriate to tribal identity, including institutions of stylised generosity and hospitality. The greatest confederation of these tribes cut across Iraq, Syria, Jordan, Saudi Arabia and Egypt/Sinai. Among these were the Aneza, the most powerful tribes in Syria, and the Shammar, though the latter were largely in Iraq after the Sykes–Picot divisions. Both were closely tied to the house of Al Saud, the ruling family in Saudi Arabia since at least the last century, through marriage – this created social and political ties which led in turn to the provision of refuge, support and salaries. Camel-raising tribes were considered the elite of these groupings, as

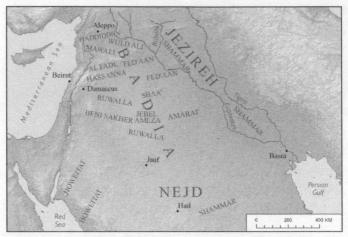

*Map of Arabia (Map prepared by Michael
Atherton, Bodleian Library, for author)*

they maintained long-range migrations that took them
deep into Arabia, where their blood ties to the house
of Al Saud meant that they had powerful protectors
during times of strife in Syria. The second rung, so to
speak, were the traditional sheep herders, who kept to
the borders of the desert and maintained close relations with the larger cities on their periphery. These
sheep-herding groups also formed themselves into
lineages and tribes and could also protect or threaten
local agricultural settlements.

Over the past sixty years many Bedouin have
settled, turning to agriculture and herding, or giving up
their herding practices altogether. The lines between
the elite and the more common tribes have begun
to blur as more camel-raising tribes turned to sheep

herding instead. By the beginning of the twenty-first century, about 15 per cent of the entire population of Syria self-identified as Bedouin. As the Syrian uprising unfolded in 2011, many of the leaders of Bedouin groups joined the peaceful demonstrations and called for greater freedoms, dignity and respect. But when the government replied with live fire, it was the Bedouin who took out their small arms – still in their possession – and began to fire back. Along a string of towns and villages from Aleppo, Hama and Homs to Deraa, Bedouin formed local self-defence units, protecting their neighbourhoods and traditional territory. At first the Assad government tried to bribe the Bedouin to stay quiet. In late summer 2011, at the end of the month of fasting (Ramadan), it was reported that the government paid individual tribesmen $100 to come out and greet Bashar al-Assad on his visit to the region near Raqqa. By 2012, many tribal leaders, like other Syrians, had left the country, but they continued to use social media – individual websites – to keep their tribesmen informed and to support their efforts to survive and resist. A tribal gathering in Mafraq, Jordan, of the main Bedouin tribal confederations, Aneza, Shammar and Baggara, and Kurdish tribes as well as Druze representatives, agreed to continue to press to protect their local rural communities and to keep services operating while at the same time opposing the Assad government.

When Syria became independent in 1943, the newly elected parliament tried to curb the powers of the Bedouin tribes. In 1956 it adopted an aggressive national policy to abolish all the tribal privileges that the French had bestowed upon the Bedouin between 1920 and 1943, during their League of Nations Mandate over the country. But the new Law of the Tribes of 1956 (Decree no. 124) continued to permit the Bedouin to carry arms in the *badia*. Land reform and government confiscation of large swathes of the *badia* saw many of the tribal leaders leaving the country for Saudi Arabia and Jordan. However, by the 1970s, Hafez al-Assad, on taking over the Baath Party in an internal coup d'état, recalled the tribal leaders who had left the decade earlier and encouraged them to return to a form of 'self-governance' in the desert areas of Syria. Over time this policy saw increasing numbers of Syrians of rural origin self-identifying as Bedouin. Belonging to a tribe was coming to be seen as impressive and important in securing protection from outsiders. With this enhanced 'self-governance', many tribes increased their movement across borders. Certainly during the years after the 2003 Anglo-American attack on Iraq, many Shammar Bedouin moved their herds and their families into Syria. The smaller, less mobile tribes moved into Lebanon and also benefited from the Syrian security presence in the Bekaa Valley of Lebanon.

As the Syrian uprising turned violent, Bedouin sought to protect their neighbourhoods and settlements using their small arms as well as new weaponry smuggled into Syria following traditional migration lines into Saudi Arabia. Bedouin tribes originally engaged with the uprising as self-defence units, but over time they began to take sides. The Aneza tribes had strong links to Saudi Arabia so largely supported the opposition to Assad's government, while the traditional sheep-herding tribes, with links to Syria's former Ministry of Interior activity in Lebanon, tended to support the government.

By 2012, forced migrants started to flood out of Syria. The Christian communities, however, largely stayed put, not feeling threatened with 'ethnic cleansing' in areas of government control. Perhaps, as well, the government had made it a point to show the world how civilised it was in the way that it protected its minority religious groups, especially its Christians. Along the southern border with Jordan, most of the forced migrants were rural and largely settled Bedouin. They were crossing the artificially created Sykes–Picot borders to seek refuge and shelter often with fellow tribesmen who were Jordanian nationals. The flight over the border to the west into Lebanon was again largely kinsmen seeking kinsmen. Many of those who fled to Lebanon had relatives or social networks in the country to help them find succour. Even on Syria's northern border the forced migration was of like to like. The first wave of migration was to the Hatay – a former region of Syria given to Turkey in 1938 while under French Mandate. Thus there was a mosaic of religious, linguistic and ethnic communities – a microcosm of Syria – Arab Alevis (Alawites), Arabic-speaking Sunnis, Turkish-speaking Sunnis,

Kurds, Turkmen, Circassians, Orthodox Christians, Jewish communities and the last surviving Armenian village in Turkey. They all had relatives in Syria and these relatives came to them seeking refuge.

The Kurds of Syria were the last to become forced migrants, largely because they protected their communities from attack successfully until 2014, when some extremist jihadi groups, along with the Islamic State, attacked Kurdish communities in both Syria and Iraq and set off an evacuation of civilians from these conflict zones. Fortunately, most Kurds have found refuge within Iraqi Kurdistan: Syrian Kurds are now refugees in the Kurdish Regional Government of Iraq; some Iraqi Kurds (Yazidis) first found refuge in Syria but have since moved on to the Kurdish Regional Government, where they have become internally displaced (IDPs). The labels may change but the ties among Kurdish communities remain.

⁞ ⁞

Both the Kurds and the Bedouin were marginalised at the end of the First World War, when the British and the French divided the Levant into spheres of influence. The Kurds were dispossessed without being moved and the Bedouin's mobility was severely curtailed. Both Kurds and Bedouin, however, were able to maintain their social cohesion through codes of behaviour and beliefs that upheld their tribal identity. As Syria collapsed into civil war, both these groups emerged stronger, protecting their communities and territories through local civil defence units and broader tribal alliances and connections with Saudi Arabia, Turkey and Iraq. The Syrian Kurdish fighters' (Peshmergas) efforts to save the Yazidi population exposed on Mount Sinjar in the summer of 2014 resulted in a great tide of public support and sympathy for Kurds in general. The Bedouin have not had such public acclaim, but their continued low-key efforts to maintain services in local communities and their brave resistance to ISIL in regions of Syria near Raqqa and Deir ez-Zor along the Euphrates River is sure to continue. Once the Iraqi Bedouin tribes of Anbar – those who fought with the US-led Awakening campaign in 2008/9 which sought to mobilise Sunni tribes against al-Qaeda – rise up against ISIL (or join the more conciliatory government of Baghdad) they will be followed by the Bedouin in Syria. Those who are in Syria today are increasingly restive. Fear is holding back some initiatives, but time is on their side and it is very likely that in the next few years a coalition of Bedouin tribes and Kurds will be a major force in bringing this episode of death and destruction in the Levant to a close. The lines drawn on the map by Sir Mark Sykes may no longer hold, but the pre-existing social and cultural groups of the Levant, with their multitude of ethno-religious belongings, will remain.

# SYRIA SEEN AND REPRESENTED

## Robin Yassin-Kassab

I'VE VISITED SYRIA twice, in June and December 2013, since the revolution erupted in the early spring of 2011. Neither visit took me to a country or a people recognisable from Western media reports.

During the first visit, I spent a week leading story-telling workshops with refugee children in the Atmeh camp, which is just inside Syria; it hugs the barbed-wire Turkish border. We were only five people – four Syrian-Americans and me – and we taught our workshops at the Return School in Atmeh. We were working in difficult conditions, dust in our mouths, in tents flapping high-volume in a hot wind, crammed in with dozens of children – girls in one aisle, boys in another – who hadn't been to school for two years, some of whom were clearly traumatised by their experience. Our workshops supplemented the labours of full-time teachers who were refugees too, and who weren't being paid.

On that first visit, it was easy to go beyond Atmeh

and deep into liberated Syria. I was frightened of the regime bombs I heard exploding in the distance, marked by the occasional plume of smoke, but not of the checkpoints operated by men in either military fatigues or tracksuits, bearded or clean-shaven, sitting under the freedom flag or Islamic banners, who smilingly waved us on. We stopped in Saraqeb, where the al-Qaeda-linked Jabhat al-Nusra was running a sharia court, and walked around unmolested – an unveiled Syrian woman (the writer Amal Hanano) was with us, and an English photographer – in the restaurants and streets. We travelled through Maaret al-Nowman to Kafranbel in Southern Idlib province – once an unheard-of backwater town, now one of Syria's revolutionary capitals – where people socialised in pool halls, cafés and private homes until the early hours of the morning, smoking, drinking tea and debating any issue that came to mind. At the media committee building, Raed Faris and others were planning and painting the slogans and cartoons for the Friday demonstration. That time the addressee was Obama (*Obama! You Send Us Weapons Only to Continue This Conflict?! Send Us Weapons to Win Our Revolution Once and for All!*), but Kafranbel's targets have included, as well as the Assad regime, the opposition's military and political leaderships, extremist Islamists, Russia and Iran, even North Korea (*Kim Jong-un! Your Attempts to Protect Assad by Diverting the World's Attention to You Is Childish: You'll Be Spanked for That!*). I sat on the terrace with activists, some local and some escaped from regime-controlled areas, visiting expatriate Syrians, including a human rights lawyer and an Italian journalist. The commander of the local Free Army militia dropped by and agreed with Raed's plan to keep weapons off the town's streets, 'for the children's sake'. I got talking with Manar Ankeer, a young man from a village further south whose entire family had fled to the Gulf. He stayed on under daily bombardment to run a free bakery that fed the villages round about.

On the terrace I shivered to the missile launchers rumbling from the regime base at Wadi Deif (the locals were very used to it and didn't once flinch). The towns we'd passed through were full of bullet holes and crumpled buildings, shutters buckled by vacuum bombs and children scarred or with missing limbs. Families who had fled from even worse towns were living with rats in demolished or half-built structures. Whether inside the country or across the borders, a journalist doesn't need a fixer to find him somebody with a story, because every single man, woman and child has a terrible tale to tell. All the horror of war and social breakdown was present and very real. Yet despite everything, this part of Syria did actually feel liberated. My visit showed me a country entirely different from the one I'd known before 2011 – because people expressed themselves freely, and criticised everything, and were struggling to build something for themselves. It was also a Syria entirely unrelated to the landscape evoked by the Western media – populated in the main not by mad-eyed jihadists or sects fated by blood to eternal warfare but by human beings in transformation, some-times truly remarkable ones.

Many of the activists I met there and later are now wanted by 'the two states' – both the Baathist and the Islamic. Pressed on all sides, these are people who have truly made history, enough to compete with and, for a moment, to drown the savage history made by states. This is the generation (working class and rural as well as bourgeois and urban, and religious as well as secular) that produced the non-sectarian freedom movement of 2011 and 2012, and that guards its prin-ciples still. These are the youths who established the Local Coordination Committees – nationally inter-linked neighbourhood cells of five or seven full-time revolutionaries each, who organised protests and work-shops to discuss the kind of society that freedom might bring. As state repression intensified, the LCCs kept count of the murdered, wounded and detained, filmed protests and regime violence, uploading these films to the internet, and provided aid to besieged areas. Later, when the state withdrew or was driven out of revolutionary areas, Revolutionary Councils were set up to administer field hospitals and basic health care, to run bakeries, to provide basic education, electricity supply, rubbish collection and so on. The concept of the LCCs and particularly the Revolutionary Councils was greatly influenced by the work of anarchist thinker Omar Aziz, who believed that radical change couldn't be brought about by protest alone, but needed the development of alternative structures to the oppressive, hierarchical state. Aziz died in regime detention in February 2013. Syria's revolutionary experiments in self-government are today beset by Assad's scorched-earth policy, by Daesh's religious brand of fascism and by the splintering of an armed opposition that is starved for arms. The focus of the councils is currently limited to community survival. Still, what they have achieved, and continue to achieve, in the most difficult of circumstances, is as worthy of celebration as it is absent from media accounts. In many councils, officials are chosen by election. These are the first real elections to have happened in Syria in half a century.

Alongside massacres and ethnic cleansing, Syrians have also experienced a veritable cultural revolution. Syrian arts are no longer delivered from the top down, from a state-sanctioned elite to a passive audience, but bottom up, or, like the LCCs organisation, horizontally. The evidence of this is in the slogans, cartoons, songs and dances of mass protest, in the graffiti and poster art, in the new hip hop and heavy metal, or in the unorthodox 'internet poetry' of Aboud Saeed and others. Most impressive is the plethora of independent TV and radio stations and the publication of more than sixty free newspapers. For instance, the women of Darayya – a suburb of Damascus subjected to siege and daily assault, where people have starved to death – produce and distribute their own newspaper, *Aneb Biladi*. The culture has also changed in terms of tribal and family relationships. Women's centres have proliferated in the liberated areas (even areas dominated by Jabhat al-Nusra); conservative women have left their homes to protest, to deliver aid and ammunition, to film and record, even to fight. Such social change, even in the midst of contrary developments, is too great to be erased.

The common belief among the Western public, fed by the media – that all sides in Syria are as bad as each other; that all opposition to Assad is inevitably extremist and sectarian – does not match the reality I and others witnessed in Syria. Engagement with revolutionaries on the ground proves there are Syrians worthy of our support; more than that, there are Syrians who could teach the rest of the world lessons in courage, intelligence and the dogged pursuit of freedom.

Most of my second visit, in December 2013, was spent on the Turkish side of the border. Our group was much bigger this time, comprising dentists, artists, photographers and football coaches, and our efforts were concentrated on the Salam School for Syrian refugees in Reyhanli, a small frontier town bustling with Syrian schools, charities and orphanages.

I managed a day's return visit to the Atmeh camp, where conditions had turned from dust to mud, from wind to snow. A child had frozen to death the night before; another had been horribly burned in a tent fire. I couldn't go any deeper into Syria because the international jihad tourists of Daesh had erected a checkpoint in Atmeh village, just beyond the camp. Six months previously camp residents had remarked on the presence of foreigners in the village. They complained that they never fought the regime, and derisively called them 'the spicy crew' in reference to their unfamiliar food. They saw them more as an amusement than a threat. But in the meantime Daesh had established mini-emirates in the north and east, and was killing Free Army commanders and revolutionary activists as well as journalists and non-Muslims. The fruits of the world's abandonment of the Syrian people were beginning to blossom.

In January 2014, a month after my visit, the entire armed opposition (the Free Syrian Army, the Islamic Front and Jabhat al-Nusra) declared war on Daesh, expelling it from Atmeh and from most of western and northern Syria. Throughout 2014 thousands of these fighters sacrificed their lives fighting Daesh, even while fending off Assad's forces. Very few people in the West are aware of this, because it was hardly reported (similarly, very few have heard of the heroic anti-Daesh resistance of the also anti-Assad Shaitat tribe, over 900 of whom have been murdered in reprisals). Nevertheless, Daesh was being steadily pushed out of Syria by revolutionary forces until its sudden success in Iraq in June, its capture of American-made Iraqi army weaponry and the money from the banks of Mosul, and then its return in force to the Syrian east.

In Atmeh camp in December 2013, the mood had definitely soured. The refugees were beginning to despair of ever going home, and a wounded sectarian identity was increasingly apparent. More people than before believed they were being attacked and driven from their homes because they were Sunnis. Why, they asked, had the Alawis remained loyal even as the regime committed genocide? Why was Shia Iran organising Assad's military effort?

It's important to recognise the sectarianism flaring in Syrian society, but it's also necessary to understand how it has been engineered. I live in Scotland, where tensions continue to simmer between the Catholic and Protestant communities, although hardly anybody goes to church, hardly anybody actively believes in God and almost nobody understands the theological distinctions between the churches. You feel the tension most on match days, when Rangers and Celtic are playing (these are Protestant and Catholic football clubs respectively), and beyond that it wasn't much of an issue. But if one day a Scottish government were to decide to deal with popular protest by sending Catholic militias into Protestant areas (or vice versa) to kill, rape and burn, very quickly churches, community centres and pubs would become targets of mutual violence. One would hope that those reporting this hypothetical conflict would recognise the immediate context, that is the divide-and-rule provocations made by those in power, and not slip into lazy stereotypes of Scots fated by history and blood to eternal religious war.

Likewise in the Middle East. In Iraq before 2003, a third of the marriages were between Sunni and Shia partners. Tribes contained both Sunni and Shia

families. The Sunni–Shia cleavage was not insurmountable, sometimes not even present; then suddenly
– as a result of political decisions – it was. And when
Hezbullah, a Lebanese Shia militia, was fighting Israel
in 2006, it was wildly popular among Syrian Sunnis.
At that point most Syrians admired Iran as a strong,
rapidly developing regional power that stood up to the
West. If some Syrians now hate Iran and its client militias, this is not the result of an eternal, unchanging
enmity. Yet far too often the media frames the Syrian
revolution and counter-revolutions as an ancient
conflict between Sunni and Shia. This orientalist
approach makes present facts irrelevant and absolves
the Assad regime and its backers from guilt.

A more attentive reading demonstrates that the
regime very deliberately, very cleverly, engineered
sectarian conflict. In the spring of 2011, at the same
time that it was targeting thousands of non-violent,
non-sectarian revolutionaries for death by torture,
the regime released the most violent and extreme of
Salafist activists from its prisons. Many of these had
fought the Americans and the Shia government in
Iraq; Assad had facilitated their passage to Iraq and
then arrested them on their return. Now they became
useful again. Many of the current leaders of Islamist
militias – Zahran Alloush of the Army of Islam, for
instance – were beneficiaries of Assad's 'amnesty'.
Meanwhile the regime relied on its own *shabiha* militias to terrorise protesting areas. In Damascus and
Aleppo, these consisted of thugs from all sectarian

backgrounds, but in the governorates of Hama, Homs and Latakia, they were selected exclusively from local Alawi and Shia communities. Very often they served as death squads. In a string of massacres in 2012, in Houla, Tremseh, Banyas and elsewhere, Alawi and Shia forces cut the throats of Sunni men, women and children.

The regime calculated rightly that a genuine reform process would end in regime dissolution; it calculated wrongly that it would win any war it provoked. The fact that it provoked this war is difficult for some Western commentators to understand, but was no secret in Syria. 'Either Assad or We Burn the Country,' the *shabiha* wrote on the walls. While the regime attacked opposition-held areas with barrel bombs, heavy artillery, scud missiles and poison gas, it pursued an undeclared non-aggression pact with Daesh until June 2014. This meant that it bombed the markets and schools of Raqqa, but not once the city's obvious Daesh HQ. The regime bought oil from Daesh, and even after it entered into battle with the jihadists, it still intervened in battles between Daesh and the Free Army – to bomb the Free Army.

Why did the regime provoke first armed resistance and then a fierce sectarian backlash? For the same reason that it once sent Salafist fanatics to Iraq: Assadist policy is to present itself as the essential solution to problems it has itself manufactured – a case of the arsonist presenting himself as fireman. The double aim of the regime's counter-revolutionary strategy was to frighten the minorities into loyalty (in particular, the drowning tyranny threw its arms around the neck of the Alawi community, making it complicit in its crimes and therefore a potential target for revenge, pulling it down with it into the depths) and the West into tolerance of the dictatorship in the face of the Islamist danger. The first has been partially successful, the second more so. Newspaper columnists and American ex-diplomats call for the West to cooperate with Assad against the jihadists, ignoring the context – Assad's far worse atrocities – which created the chaos in which jihadism thrives.

Media pundits have asserted, and perhaps much of the public in the West believes, that the United States and its allies have supported the Syrian opposition and its revolution. This is simply not true. Weeks into the mass killing of unarmed protesters, US Secretary of State Hillary Clinton was describing Assad as a reformer. Later on, the US and Europe sent selected Free Army brigades ready-meals, a few uniforms, some satellite phones and so on. Later still, some light weapons were delivered, even some anti-tank arms, but only sporadically. Syrian fighters describe it as the tap being turned on and then off again as soon as any progress is made. For a long time the only American move that actually made a difference was to veto other powers from supplying the anti-aircraft weapons essential to defend liberated areas from Assad's planes. American policy has been fairly consistent: to encourage Assad to stand down while keeping the regime – expanded to include a few safe oppositional faces – in place. It's a policy that fundamentally misunderstands the nature of both regime and revolution, that is morally bankrupt, and that allows jihadism to bloom. In the name of 'realism', Assad was permitted to raze the areas beyond his control and displace 10 million from their homes. In the name of disengagement, American planes are now bombing both Syria and Iraq, and Jabhat al-Nusra and Ahrar al-Sham, both Islamist opposition groups, as well as Daesh. They aren't bombing Assad; indeed Assad's and Obama's planes share the sky. The immediate result of this on the ground has been a surge of support for Daesh and, much more, for Jabhat al-Nusra.

Who has sent weaponry to the Syrian opposition? Saudi Arabia has armed militias with tribal connec-tions to the Kingdom, some secular and some moderate Islamist. Saudi individuals have also donated to Daesh – but not the state itself, which is terrified of the jihadist threat, and which recently gave $1 billion to the Lebanese army to defend Lebanon against Daesh incursions. The Qataris have funded Islamist but not transnational jihadist groups. Neither the Saudi nor the Qatari rulers are interested in democracy (both monarchies sent troops to crush the democratic uprising in Bahrain), though they may be genuinely outraged by the damage done to Syria. Turkey has passed a small amount of weaponry to the Free Army, but its political role in housing the now largely irrel-evant Syrian National Coalition has been more impor-tant. Turkey has been the most generous of neighbours in permitting Syrian charities and political activity to operate on its territory, and allowing free passage of refugees and fighters. Very damagingly, however, it has until recently also allowed the free passage of foreign jihadists. I crossed the border illegally on my June visit. The Kurdish boys who led me across – right next to the official border post – told me they'd brought Chechens on the same route. Perhaps Turkey was motivated by the desire to pressure Syria's Kurds, or perhaps its crimes of omission arise from mere incompetence. In any case, they are now likely to rebound on the Turkish state and people.

Put together, the external arming and funding of the Syrian revolution has been done far too little, in an uncoordinated way, and is subject to American veto. This has guaranteed the failure of the Free Army to develop into a coherent, well-disciplined structure. Instead the free militias squabble over a tiny pool of aid while the jihadists grow.

These facts do not seem to perturb many of the 'liberal-left' (I use inverted commas because their inane positions are neither liberal nor leftist), despite the clear principle that people who suffer genocidal acts and ethnic cleansing have the right to defend themselves, and the right to take weapons from anywhere they can.

Much of the 'left' (Britain's Stop the War Coalition comes to mind) have read the Syrian revolution from the start as an imperialist plot to unseat a socialist resistance regime, part of the 'war on terror' process, a rerun of Iraq. But Syria, and indeed our world, is much more complicated when seen from the ground. The line of thought that offers a 'left' justification for Assad is undisturbed by the contradictions of a 'socialism' in which one man – the president's cousin Rami Makhlouf – controls 60 per cent of the economy, in which neo-liberalism has pauperised vast segments of the population; or of an 'anti-Zionist resistance' which slaughtered Palestinians in Lebanon in the 1980s and in Yarmouk camp today, which hasn't fired a single bullet across the occupied Golan Heights since 1973. Most important, its ill-fitting Iraq analogy ignores the fact that there is no American occupation in Syria, and there was no popular revolution in Iraq.

Iranian and Russian support for the Assad regime is too often not interrogated by anti-war activists in the West. In the face of our century's greatest crimes, the media has too often retreated into absurd conspiracy theories. The most distasteful examples were Seymour Hersh's articles in the *London Review of Books* blaming Assad's August 2013 sarin gas attacks on resistance-held Damascus suburbs (which killed up to 2,000 people) on the resistance itself, in cooperation with the Turkish government. This improbable theory was based on one unnamed source and was comprehensively debunked (Eliot Higgins and Muhammad Idrees Ahmad did the best jobs); for many on the left it has nevertheless attained the status of gospel truth.

Others wonder from a distance if the revolution was wise – as if it happened by collective decision rather than as the result of a failing system's inevitable collapse – and condemn the decision to militarise, which in actuality was not one but a million individual decisions taken under fire. Perhaps worst of all, the idea is promoted, explicitly or not, that the Arabs are such a benighted people, so naturally prone to violent dissension, that they are better off under the rule of a strong man. The chaos expanding in Syria is therefore the fault of the treasonous or naive youngsters who stood up to state terror. This notion inverts logical, chronological and moral order. It is akin to the arguments that blame Jewish behaviour for German anti-Semitism, Palestinian behaviour for Zionist oppression or women's behaviour when men beat or rape them.

It's a tragedy that Syrians have been so misrepresented in their hour of heroism and need. It's another, directly related, tragedy that the world's states, by omission and commission, have abandoned not only Syrians but their own peoples as well to a future of destabilisation and terror. The hope lies in Syrians themselves, and those who learn from them, those who will continue to forge a new type of history.

# DEFYING THE KILLERS: THE EMERGENCE OF STREET CULTURE IN SYRIA

## Malu Halasa

### 1

Taken on their own, graffiti, low-resolution pixelated camerawork and Arabic slang may not appear to be socially transformative. However, together their impact has had profound implications in Syria, where the cultural revolution that accompanied a broader political uprising is perhaps the only positive development in over four years of brutal conflict.

Syrian activists were not operating in a vacuum. For many young Syrians, developments in Egypt and Tunisia were a call to artistic action. In the early months of 2011, a calligrapher in the countryside outside Hama and a fine arts student in Damascus were designing posters and uploading them on the internet for Egyptian and Tunisian activists to carry in their demonstrations. Soon bloody events closer to home prompted Syrians to initiate similar activities for their country. Through the internet, with Syrians inside and outside the country, an anonymous poster collective, known as Alshaab alsori aref tarekh ('The Syrian People Know Their Way') created posters that demonstrators downloaded from Flickr and other social media sites and carried during the first year of the Syrian marches.[1]

Graffiti was another form of street art that crossed borders quickly.[2] To a large extent, Syrians were influenced by the plethora of overtly political images and statements that appeared in the squares of Tunis and Cairo after January 2011. Egypt's street artist El Teneen would repay the compliment several months later with a stencil showing Bashar al-Assad's head sporting Hitler's distinct hairline and moustache that spread across social networks.

In Syria, graffiti launched the uprising. It was not the face of a political figure but a slogan popularised in the heat of nearby revolutions. 'Al-shaab yurid isqat al-nizam' ('The People Want to Bring Down the Regime') was spray-painted by fifteen schoolboys on a wall in the town of Deraa on 6 March 2011. Until this point, Syrians had not yet demanded the overthrow of the Assad family's forty-year-long dictatorship, only the easing of the Emergency Law and the granting of greater political freedoms. However, the arrest and subsequent torture of the schoolboys, followed by the shooting of unarmed demonstrators on the streets of Deraa, acted as a catalyst for further mass demonstrations. These quickly spread to Homs, Hama, Baniyas and Damascus, and paved the way for a social and artistic activism never before seen in the country.

As the artist, cinematographer and writer Khalil Younes described it, it was 'the revolution within the revolution'.

By that summer, as attacks and massacres by the *shabiha* regime-controlled thugs continued unabated, Damascus became a canvas for engaged art interventions. In particular people discovered that the most powerful weapon against a totalitarian dictatorship is ridicule. Activists turned the water in public fountains red. Hundreds of ping-pong balls carrying messages of freedom and dignity were released on Mount Qasiun, some of which rolled on to the grounds of Bashar al-Assad's palace.

Near official buildings or heavily patrolled public squares, loudspeakers hidden on rooftops, in trashcans or treetops blared out the sounds of protest marches, which sent the Syrian *mukhabarat*, or secret police, scurrying. As one unnamed artist-activist explained, 'Because we don't have weapons, this kind of uprising is more intensive than an armed struggle. We want to affect the security forces, make them nervous, but we also want to suggest something smart, interactive and jokey.'

The spontaneous mass demonstrations that took place in the cities in the country's north were 'carnivalesque' in the Bakhtinian sense of challenging authority and allowing transgressive ideas to flourish. In the city of Hama, the site of a brutal massacre by Hafez al-Assad (Bashar's father) in 1982, the crowd of thousands singing along to fireman and local singer

Qashoush's wittily chanted verses from 'Yalla irhal ya Bashar!' ('Come on, Bashar, get out!') was cathartic. In Homs, when the regime checkpoints prevented people from entering the main clock tower square to demonstrate, they constructed their own miniature clock towers and processed around those.

Kafranbel, a previously unheard-of hamlet, emerged as a new centre for Syrian sardonic humour. Anonymous local illustrators and town wits garnered international acclaim for hand-drawn editorial cartoons and immaculately lettered protest banners authored as 'Occupied Kafranbel' or, by 2013, 'Syrian Revolution – Kafranbel'. To this day, photos of these images held up by the town's young men signal collective responsibility for the sentiments expressed.

In another setting, activists from the Kartoneh collective who remained in war-destroyed Deir ez-Zor used the familiar and neutral iconography of traffic symbols, tinged with mordant humour. For example, two cars side by side in a red circle told residents 'No overtaking' the goal of 'Citizenship, Justice and Equality' for all; or a road narrowing ahead sign, which warned that there are only two choices – either opposition or pro-regime. The activists' aim was to create a non-sectarian signage that would galvanise people of varying religious and ethnic backgrounds remaining in the city. According to a collective member, they may have had 7,000 followers on Facebook, yet more than 390,000 people have shared or seen their posters.

Artistic activity by ordinary people came about,

so said the country's best-known editorial cartoonist, Ali Ferzat, because the barrier of fear erected and enforced by the dictatorship, had been broken. For decades, Ferzat published heavily metaphorical editorial cartoons critical of the state in the government-operated newspaper *Al-Thawra* ('The Revolution').[3] In 2011, after he shifted from symbolic drawings to produce more explicitly targeted caricatures of Assad, Ferzat was attacked by outraged regime supporters and fled to Kuwait.

Cartoons and comic strips had featured regularly in official Baath Party children's magazines for decades. However, for a new generation of Syrian illustrators, graphic designers and animators – some with backgrounds in fine art, advertising or film storyboarding – it was not the country's official cartooning culture or Ferzat's coded messages that inspired them. They found modern subversive narratives by reading Japanese Manga online in English translation.

Like the political posters of The Syrian People Know Their Way collective, Comic4Syria strips were uploaded on the group's Facebook page for domestic and international consumption. They too documented the main events, themes and aspirations of the uprising. But the comic strips served an internal and sometimes critical purpose alongside their obvious storytelling. When the opposition Free Syrian Army was accused of torturing its prisoners, Comic4Syria produced leaflets distributed by activists which drew on the humane treatment of prisoners called for in the Qur'an.

Sumud (*Steadfastness*) by Comic4Syria, 2012, *appears*
*courtesy of the anonymous comic strip collective*

2

Alongside the anonymous young, Syria's best-known painter, Youssef Abdelke, created the Facebook page Art and Freedom (art.liberte.syrie), where artists posted their work on the condition that they signed their names to show solidarity with the revolution. The website served as a counter to Syria's small but formal gallery culture, where the more established art spaces would not have been able to operate without tacit approval from the government. Art and Freedom also narrowed the gap between what is considered 'art', whether from the academy or the cartoonist's pen. However, distinctions like that were not made by the *mukhabarat* and Abdelke, like Ali Ferzat, was treated as a threat. Last summer, the artist disappeared at a government checkpoint and was held incommunicado for a couple of months.

An early indication that Syrians were formulating a highly unique creative approach to depicting and understanding the conflict was the 2011–12 staggered release on YouTube and Vimeo of *Top Goon: Diaries of a Little Dictator* by the anonymous artists' collective Masasit Mati, named for the straw used by Syrians to drink the popular herbal tea, maté, now largely unavailable due to sanctions. In two seasons of thirty-four episodes, seen by over 1 million viewers on Facebook, an all-powerful president was reduced to the lisping, large-nosed finger puppet Beeshu, the Top Goon, often embroiled in Punch and Judy-type squabbles with a character named Shabih (Goon). Humour can defuse fear in the darkest hour. And for when it's too hard to deal with, Masasit Mati quoted Nietzsche as guidance: 'Be careful when you fight the monsters, lest you become one.' If the message was too important to miss, the puppeteers came out from behind the curtain – their faces masked – and addressed the camera (and the audience) directly.

For many on the streets of Syria, truth had become stranger than the imagination. Ordinary Syrians started filming events using any recording device at hand – mobile phones, digital cameras and crap laptops – to address what they saw as the enormous gap between regime propaganda on state-run TV channels and their own day-to-day reality. Since 2011, Syria's impressive citizen-journalist movement has posted over 300,000 short films and reports on the internet. The scope of the footage broadened as the movement became equipped with phones with better cameras and all manner of spy cameras through the organising efforts of the nationwide Local Coordinating Committees. Some of it included intimate scenes of torture filmed in claustrophobic settings by spy cameras. Sometimes, even more chillingly, the torturers themselves posted the footage as trophy imagery.

Showing short, sharp fragments, devoid of a wider context, was not enough for a growing number of anonymous documentary film-maker collectives. These include DOX BOX (now working as the Proaction production company), Abounaddara and Bidayyat Audiovisual Arts, which started posting short films showing interviews or diary reports. News, shorts and feature-length films from Syria were no longer the preserve of media outlets or aspiring movie-makers; it was something that anyone could do, regardless of background, experience or even equipment. Often the most powerful imagery was low-resolution, heavily pixelated and blurred.

Again these developments on Syrian streets were not without danger. Some films showed the death of a camera-person after he or she had been shot by the sniper who had been filmed by the camera. Like the disputed Iranian elections of 2009, which spawned the failed Green Movement, the still or moving camera served the function of a spy on the street. The authorities had declared war and realism, gritty and otherwise, became an enemy of the state.

3

The rise of the street has also been mirrored in the language emerging from Arab revolutions. Syrian writer and broadcaster Rana Kabbani noted the increased use of slang and colloquial Arabic in the postings on Facebook and Twitter. This language entered the chat room and allowed for a larger liberation in terms of who could express themselves. Instead of being forced to rely on Modern Standard Arabic, the formal language, grammar and approach of 'proper' public discourse across the Middle East, people were suddenly expressing themselves in the everyday manner in which they spoke and thought.

This informality also encouraged the unbridled public airing of once-taboo subjects for the first time – sometimes if only for their shock value.

Before 2011, twenty-something Muslim Syrians used euphemisms to vent their frustrations in public. Derogatory words or sexual slang were not considered polite or acceptable language in a traditional society firmly anchored by family and conservative social mores. Social media provided a platform for more explicit views. Last year one activist wrote 'dick bitch' on his Facebook page twenty times and then added, 'Now do I have your attention? Four hundred people died in Syria today.'

The internet has always encouraged slang and abbreviated writing in English and other languages; Arabic would prove no different. Last year saw the publication of *The Smartest Guy on Facebook: Status Updates from Syria* by Aboud Saeed, a former blacksmith who left school when he was in the ninth grade. Described as 'the Syrian Bukowski', Saeed found his own free space in the ruptures of his society. His wide-ranging topics included his traditional henna-tattooed mother – 'My mom has never been to Tibet, she's never worn a bikini and doesn't know how to sit on a toilet' – to existential musings – 'Is there less death on Twitter?'

Saeed's flippancy was all the more significant considering his location. Manbij, near Aleppo, currently under Islamic State rule, also featured in a short documentary by Masasit Mati not released as part of the *Top Goon* episodes. Entitled *I Love Acting*, it tells the story of a 2013 cultural festival painstakingly planned by activists in the town that was disrupted after Manbij was shelled by the regime the day before and several people were killed.

You don't have to be male and working class to write edgy prose. Established short-story writer Rasha Abbas, with a background in Syrian television, uses fiction to affirm the value of the individual amid the collectivist barbarities of the conflict. As her translator, Alice Guthrie, described Abbas's most recent collection, tentatively entitled *The Gist of It*, 'Eclectic, intense, often psychedelic, many of her stories are dreamscapes which creep up on the reader with sudden plunges into haunting hyper-realism, operating within a punk aesthetic.'[4]

Another Syrian in exile, Khalil Younes, was one of the first artists to emerge with a distinct style, showing the Syrian revolution through bold pen and ink drawings initially of martyrs. As his series continued, his portraits included metaphorical figures that represented massacres or representations from other wars. 'Our Saigon Execution', for instance, transfers Eddie Adams's famous 1968 photograph of the shooting of a Vietcong officer to the Syrian situation.

Younes, who grew up in the alleys of Damascus, has been posting short stories from forty to 400 words on the internet. He maintained that many of the new Syrian writers are writing short as opposed to long because short stories are better adapted for reading on smart phones and tablets. Younes also belongs to a group of artists who, in the early days, acted as a bridge between untutored 'arters' and the West, where Younes has been living since 1998.[5]

This professional group of artists discouraged less sophisticated images of, for example, naked children's bums as a metaphor for circumstances in Syria. They discussed with their fellow citizens the kind of visual material that could more strongly affect and appeal to international audiences schooled in advertising and contemporary art. The internet and social media may give the impression that the featured art and culture were posted spontaneously. In fact, much exploration, experimentation and editing have gone into producing polished, engaging and powerful imagery and text.

# 4

When Masasit Mati snuck back into Syria to perform with the finger puppets and filmed *I Love Acting*, the director Jameel (a pseudonym) said they had to be careful of being caught not only by the regime but by the newly dominant Islamic militias. 'They don't like theatre,' he observed succinctly.

In November 2014, the photographer and film director Ziad Homsi was kidnapped in Raqqa by IS and suddenly released over two weeks later. He is best known as the co-director of *Notre Terrible Pays* ('Our Terrible Country'), with Ali Atassi and produced by Bidayyat. Homsi is an active member of Lens Young, unofficial groups of citizen-photographers documenting Syria's destruction. Increasingly, artists were critical of the Islamist forces as well as the regime. However, since the rise of the Islamic State (IS) in Syria and Iraq, cultural resistance has had to be highly secretive.

Cameras can't be openly brought on to the streets, so they are invariably hidden under a niqab face-covering. Last September, an anonymous woman activist filmed public life in Raqqa with a hidden camera. During the short film, two men in a car scolded her for not fully covering her face. In another scene, shot in an internet café, a French-speaking jihadist bride tells her sobbing mother over Skype that she is not coming home. So was the film, broadcast on the TV channel France 2, an example of engaged culture or an exercise in straight-up reporting? Or was it the revenge of a street that should have been kept hidden, docile and uncomplaining – like the Syrian street under Assad, which had been known for its vibrancy in manufacturing and design but for the most part was silent, while politically critical in private but very rarely in public. In the areas inside Syria where IS hold sway, the barrier of fear once the preserve of the regime has again been erected by the jihadists.

Realism as well as satire appears to be a tall order for IS, which will behead anyone caught filming.[6] It would be mistaken to blame the strict fundamental version of the religion that the militia purports to follow, where human representation is not allowed. In a political movement as savvy as theirs in its use of social media, their motivations have more to do with control and mission-branding. Their threatening communiqués demanding ransom or showing gruesome beheadings have been made to either strike fear into the heart of their enemies or appeal to disaffected radicalised youth around the world. Unlike the art, film-making, culture and writing of the Syrian uprising, these are messages that entirely disallow creative expression, contestation or dissent.

Despite the violence, disruption and threat of arrest of 2014, the country played host to the first ever Syria's Mobile Phone Films Festival, organised by activists and the Alshare3 ('The Street') Foundation, which works across the arts – film, music and visual arts. Ten short films made by Syrians vied in four categories for prizes of $1,000 each. Festival organisers were planning to hold simultaneous screenings at various locations inside the country. Kobane was intended to be one of the towns, but fighting between IS and Peshmerga forces forced them to cancel. After that, the festival responded flexibly and revealed the time and place of its screenings on Facebook or locally. Sometimes the choice of venue had a particularly powerful resonance, like Jabal al-Zawiya, the site of a major 2011 massacre by soldiers. After years of mutual destruction, Syrians came to the festival to be reminded of the best of themselves.

*Graffiti on a wall inside Syria: 'Has to be Freedom!
Come to the Street.' Kafranbel, 2013*

## Postscript

The book Zaher Omareen, Nawara Mafoud and I
edited, *Syria Speaks: Art and Culture from the Frontline*, featuring over fifty Syrian contributors and much
of the material discussed in this essay, serves a similar
function. At a time of continuing violence – from the
regime, Islamist forces, US air strikes and much more
the voices and aspirations of ordinary Syrians obscured
by repressive authoritarian rule are finally reaching
audiences inside and outside the country.[7]

During last winter's staged performance, entitled
'Readings from *Syria Speaks*', musically illustrated
stories from the book were presented alongside as
yet unpublished work. The sell-out audience laughed
during the darkly humorous passages and seemingly

held their breath as the subject matter turned grim. If the articulate, often hilarious and elegiac Syrian voices are heard, real lives emerge – not victims or war statistics – from a conflict that has wasted a country. The power of Syria remains in people's memories, aspirations and poignant sense of irony and beauty. The metaphorical 'street' can be anywhere; it has the power to sustain even those who are living in exile.

Last year, Syria's best known-novelist, Khaled Khalifa, came from Damascus for the *Syria Speaks* book tour. At a literary workshop in Bristol, Khalifa slipped outside for a cigarette, only to be joined by a group of Syrian asylum seekers. By coincidence they were all from the same rural Kurdish Syrian village surrounded by olive groves where the author had grown up. As they gathered around him, they asked about the trees and the harvest.

# AFTERWORD

# PALESTINE AND HOPE

## Raja Shehadeh

THE MIDDLE EAST of my youth was a very different place from what it is now. In a small instance of an issue that looms large in the cultural politics of today, I don't remember hearing a discussion about whether women should wear the hijab. Whether or not a woman chose to wear a headscarf was a personal choice, not done to impress or even necessarily to indicate religious affiliation. Many older Christian women wore a scarf just like their Muslim counterparts, while middle-class urban Muslim girls, like their Christian friends, snuck lipstick and tried to wear their skirts as short as possible – a practice I would have encouraged had I not been such a shy teenager. We, Christians and Muslims, observed each other's holy days. These were occasions of celebration and neighbourly competition – but mostly over the most tasty food on offer. Of course there was prejudice – I grew up in a small town, after all – but our jokes about people from Hebron, the fecklessness of the Lebanese or the family down the street that consistently produced drunkards were relatively harmless.

However, it was not as though these times were not difficult and even dark. Growing up in the shadow of the Palestinian Nakba of 1948 – I was born in 1951, after my parents had fled Jaffa for the West Bank town of Ramallah – I spent the first sixteen years of my life under Jordanian rule. Palestinians had no political freedom and freedom of speech was scant indeed. My outspoken father spent some months in a Jordanian desert prison called El Jafer. It was a harsh experience for him, but nothing like what was to come. The same prison was used after 9/11 for extraordinary rendition, the CIA-sponsored secret detention and interrogation, often accompanied by torture, of 'extrajudicial' suspects.

When my family travelled overland to Lebanon through Jordan and Syria, as we did every summer in the late 1950s and early 1960s, we had to cross a number of borders and were given a difficult time. The army ruled in Syria and the security services justified their severity by the need to be strong and vigilant in face of the Israeli enemy looming at the border. My parents had friends whose children had disappeared in Syrian jails after being tortured. We were stopped for hours at the borders and held our breath, knowing that we were going through a country with a repressive regime and had to be careful what we said and how we behaved. All this excessive concentration on the military and security was supposed to be for our own good as Palestinians, for the Arab countries were preparing for the coming war against Israel and the eventual liberation of our usurped land, Palestine, and the return of the refugees. Writing of his country, Egypt, in this volume, Khaled Fahmy observes that 'not only has the century-long Arab–Israeli conflict sapped our energy and diverted precious resources, but our despots have also used it cynically to postpone indefinitely democratic reforms'.

When, after a long and trying eight hours crammed in a hot car, we finally arrived in Beirut the atmosphere seemed different. There was a measure of freedom of expression, as well as a greater variety of religious faiths and affiliations that seemed to coexist side by side, including a small Jewish community whose members operated a number of celebrated shops on the famous Hamra Street.

In Palestine and the several Arab countries I experienced, there seemed to be an acceptance that religious practice and observance was a personal choice. There was generally tolerance and acceptance of the different faiths. Yes, there were fanatics, zealots and just pure crazies – Palestine has had its share of all these throughout history. But for the rest of us, political hardships could not be blamed on religion.

In 1967 the long-awaited war with Israel took place: the ensuing disaster changed everything. In the words of Israeli general and Minister of Defence Moshe Dayan, Israel now became an empire. Israel was on the march, colonising more of the occupied

Palestinian territories through building Jewish settlements and doing all that was possible to encourage the Palestinians to leave. And yet if the Arab armies had proved highly ineffective in liberating Palestine, their failure did not sever the emotional link between the rest of the Arabs and those suffering under Israeli rule.

Not only did the Arab world follow the travails of the Palestinians with a profound sense of frustration; it watched in bewilderment the successes of the Israelis, including their effective use of the media to impress on the world Israel's own mythical and exclusive version of the history of our country. No less disturbing to the ordinary Palestinians and Arabs was the biased, indeed unfettered, support of the United States and Western Europe for Israel, whatever violations of international law it was committing.

After the 1967 defeat, many Palestinians joined the Palestine Liberation Organisation in its political and military struggle against Israel. The less political, like myself, thought that the struggle for human rights and international law could also open new avenues for justice for Palestine. Both these paths had resonance in the rest of the Arab world: the absence of the rule of law and democracy in many Arab countries had to be addressed. As contributors to this volume have observed, the Arab states, in their colonial origins and their development, have been marked by a lack of legitimacy and a failure to be representative of, or accountable to, their people.

It took many years before the struggle that the

unarmed Palestinians in the Occupied West Bank and Gaza waged against the Israeli army, the strongest in the Middle East, served as an inspiration to the Arab masses, first in Tunisia and then in Egypt. The Arab Spring that began in January 2011 was a time of hope that democracy might be finally sweeping the region. I was transfixed by the power of ordinary people to make change. Several essays in this book described how the revolutions that occurred in the Middle East region released the creativity among the populations of these places that had long been in abeyance. Malu Halasa described how the people of Syria used the internet, cartoons, drama and video to give voice to the Syrian popular opposition, and she also notes the links that emerged between the Syrian poster artists and those of Egypt. There too street art, which had long been prohibited, flourished. If anything this confirms how indomitable is the human spirit. For decades the people of Syria and Egypt have endured oppressive regimes that stifled all forms of creative expression and yet their spirit and aspiration for freedom could not be extinguished. It also indicates how quickly change can happen.

Four years later, looking around me, listening to the news and travelling through the region, I constantly realise how much it has changed almost beyond recognition. Despair is now the dominant sentiment and optimism is in short supply. Like others, I sometimes feel paralysed by the horrors ordinary people have had to endure now in Syria, Iraq and Egypt.

From the perspective of occupied Palestine, where

I live, the shared taxi ride from Ramallah to Jerusalem tells a larger story of our journey through all these difficult decades to our crisis-ridden present. Part of the story is obvious: the increased physical obstacles and denials of freedom of movement that have made this short journey of ten miles a Palestinian nightmare. But the ride also evokes the political and psychological climate. As a teenager, I always enjoyed riding in a shared taxi, the *servees*, or the bus, on the journey to Jerusalem. Everyone spoke to everyone else. It is true we all kept away from politics, but there were jokes told, stories shared and loud happy music played. How different it was then, and not simply in the absence of checkpoints and an annexation wall, but also arriving to see Jerusalem's pastoral beauty, now vanquished by the highways and bridges criss-crossing it, connecting the Jewish settlements to the east with the western Jewish part of the city while largely erasing the Arab part of the city. Later, during the 1980s and particularly during the first Palestinian intifada, the *servees* served as our Facebook, exchanging news of coming demonstrations and past arrests and tales of our young 'generation of stones'. During the hard times of the second intifada, passengers and driver simply tried to get to their destination, discussing whether a route through an olive grove or a stone quarry would serve. Today, the passengers are mostly silent in the long wait at checkpoints. What is there to say? Sometimes a taxi driver pontificates with a sigh, 'Our struggle with the Jews is eternal, so says the Holy Qur'an.' The small talk that was common and the joyful music that was played have turned to total silence, with everyone lost in their own dim thoughts or concentrating on listening to the Qur'anic readings and recitations coming from the radio. I would attribute this less to an embrace of piety than a loss of hope. So, is there hope for Palestine and the Middle East?

I still believe that there is, but only if the core problem, the Palestinian problem, is resolved on grounds that allow equality between Israelis and Palestinians and for the Palestinians to enjoy their own state. Only then could the deadly fuse that was ignited more than a hundred years ago and which has been slowly burning further and further afield, setting off many bombs along its route over the large region of the Middle East, be extinguished. Only then could calm return and with it hope for a better future. But in our crisis-ridden times, it is also clear to me that the foundations of a solution to the question of Palestine – equality and an end to exclusivity – must also underlie a new vision of our whole region.

The possibility would then arise for movement between, and cooperation among, the countries of the region. The Middle East is not meant to be fragmented. As the essays in this book have shown, this was the doing of the colonial powers after the First World War. The different parts of the region comple-ment each other and would derive huge benefits in every sphere from the interaction between them. In some there is capital, in others labour. Here

entrepreneurial spirit, there a wealth of business experience. Here empty land, there congestion. Here an
excess of educated people, there a need for teachers
and professionals. Here excess wealth and run-away
consumption; there enormous needs for investment in
people and infrastructure. From the interaction would
arise many benefits from a rich cultural and religious
mix, bringing a new cosmopolitanism rooted in our
history. The region would go back to acting as the
bridge between East and West as it has done for many
centuries in the past.

None of this can happen as long as the borders
remain closed, as long as the Palestinian–Israeli conflict
is not resolved and the security of Israel is used as an
excuse to continue Western military interventions and
restrictions on the people of the region. But this is not
all. Much also depends on how the other issues that
are troubling the region are understood.

The Islamic State of Iraq and the Levant (ISIL)
seems to thrive on the frustration of people facing
seemingly insurmountable obstacles in their fight for
greater rights and freedom within their own states and
the failure of the Palestinians to win the liberation of
their land occupied by Israel over four decades earlier
through the reliance on peaceful resistance and invoca-
tion of the rule of law. The cause of law, whether municipal or international, as a vehicle for peaceful change
and transformation was also not furthered by the wide
definition US law gave to terrorism that rendered legitimate resistance to occupation and oppression as illegal.

ISIL seems to have learned dangerous and brutal lessons from the repeated failure of Arab states and armies in their fight against Israel and the Western powers: how to manipulate the media perhaps from Israel's noted success, how to be cured of illusions about the democracy of the West from the actions of the West itself. Discredited rhetoric about the rule of law and democracy – and the absence of both in the Arab regimes the West has supported – both undermines the states ISIL challenges and leaves people without these powerful tools to fight their own battles against ISIL barbarism. These lessons and legacies are proving chillingly effective in ISIL's control of the Syrian and Iraqi territories it has conquered.

Speaking to the BFM TV in the wake of the January 2015 attacks in France that killed seventeen people, the former French prime minister Dominique de Villepin, who led the opposition to the Iraq War, described the Islamic State as the 'deformed child' of Western policy. He wrote in *Le Monde* that the West's wars in the Muslim world 'nourish terrorism among us with promises of eradicating it'. His analysis was right, as was his warning against simplifying these conflicts in the Middle East by 'seeing only the Islamist symptom'. It is hoped that this book will have made it possible for readers to better understand the issues at stake in the Middle East and to think beyond simplistic paradigms and sound bites.

As the authors of the essays here have ably demonstrated, writers have an important role to play in bringing about change, not only by analysing what is taking place but also by imagining how things could be different. In this way writers can ultimately tilt the balance and encourage the victory of those with positive creative energy over those who espouse the negative energy of terror and violence. These essays have demonstrated that the energy of creation is still alive, whether in Egypt, Syria or Iraq, even in the darkest of times and the seemingly most desperate of places.

# NOTES

**The Significance of a Screwdriver: Penny Johnson**

1. See Patrick Cockburn, *The Jihadis Return: ISIS and the New Sunni Uprising* (New York, OR Books, 2014), p. 10.
2. Mouin Rabbani, 'The Un-Islamic State', Norwegian Peacebuilding Resource Centre, September 2014.
3. Slavoj Žižek, *The Year of Dreaming Dangerously* (London, Verso Books, 2012), p. 35.

**The Post-Ottoman Syndrome: Avi Shlaim**

1. T. E. Lawrence, *Revolt in the Desert* (London, Jonathan Cape, 1927).
2. George Antonius, *The Arab Awakening: The Story of the Arab National Movement* (New York, Capricorn Books, 1938), p. 248.
3. Elie Kedourie, *England and the Middle East: The Destruction of the Ottoman Empire, 1914–1921* (London, Bowes and Bowes, 1956), pp. 212–13.
4. Quoted without an indication of the author in Pierre Salinger with Eric Laurent, *Secret Dossier: The Hidden*

*Agenda behind the Gulf War* (London, Penguin Books, 1991), p. 14.

5.  Quoted in Michael L. Dockrill and Douglas J. Goold, *Peace Without Promise: Britain and the Peace Conferences, 1919–1923* (London, Batsford, 1981), pp. 163–4.

6.  Quoted in David Fromkin, *A Peace to End All Peace: Creating the Modern Middle East, 1914–1922* (London, Penguin Books, 1989), p. 5.

## The Divisive Line: James Barr

1.  British Library, Add. 63039, Bertie to Grey, 30 November 1915.

2.  David Garnett (ed.), *The Letters of T. E. Lawrence* (London, Jonathan Cape, 1938), pp. 193–4, Lawrence to Hogarth, 18 March 1915.

3.  W. Crooke, review of *The Caliph's Last Heritage* in *Man*, Vol. 17, January 1917, p. 24.

4.  Sudan Archive, Durham, Wingate Papers 135/6, Sykes to Callwell, 1915.

5.  Colonel R. Meinertzhagen, *Middle East Diary, 1917–1936* (London, Cresset Press, 1959), p. 26.

## Why Did You Rename Your Son? Salim Tamari

1.  Najib Nassar and Hanna Abu Hanna, *Riwayat Mifleh al-Ghassani: aw, Safhah min safahatt al-harb al-'alamiyah* (al-Nasirah, Dar al-Sawt, 1981).

2.  Salim Tamari, 'With God's Camel in Siberia: The Russian Exile of an Ottoman Officer from Jerusalem', *Jerusalem Quarterly*, Vol. 35, 2008, p. 35.

3.  See Salim Tamari, *The Year of the Locust: A Soldier's Diary and the Erasure of the Ottoman Past* (Berkeley, CA, University of California Press, 2011), p. 91.

## A Long View from Baghdad: Justin Marozzi

1. See www.theguardian.com/world/2003/feb/19/iraq. artsandhumanities.

2. Hanna Batatu, *The Old Social Classes and the Revolutionary Movements of Iraq: A Study of Iraq's Old Landed and Commercial Classes and of Its Communists, Ba'athists and Free Officers* (London, Saqi Books, 2004), p. 25.

3. Maha Yahya, 'Iraq's Existential Crisis: Sectarianism Is Just Part of the Problem', Carnegie Middle East Center, 6 November 2014. See carnegie-mec.org/2014/11/06/ iraq-s-existential-crisis-sectarianism-is-just-part-of-problem.

4. Jita Mishra, *The NPT and the Developing Countries* (New Delhi, Concept Publishing Company, 2008), p. 156.

5. 'UN Says Sanctions Have Killed Some 500,000 Iraqi Children', Reuters report, 21 July 2000. See www. commondreams.org/headlines/072100–03.htm.

6. Paul Roberts, *The Demonic Comedy: Some Detours in the Baghdad of Saddam Hussein* (Farrar, Straus and Giroux, New York, 1997), p. 214.

7. Yahya, 'Iraq's Existential Crisis'.

## Iran: Coming in from the Cold? Ramita Navai

1. See www.nytimes.com/2014/10/28/world/middleeast/ human-rights-in-iran-have-worsened-un-investigator-says.html.

2. See globalvoicesonline.org/2014/09/16/nearly-70-percent-of-young-iranians-use-illegal-internet-circumvention-tools/.

3. See www.salon.com/2015/01/15/

why_porn_is_exploding_in_the_middle_
east_partner/?utm_source=facebook&utm_
medium=socialflow.

## Living and Writing in Kuwait: Mai al-Nakib

1. Edward W. Said, *Representations of the Intellectual* (New York, Pantheon Books, 1994), p. 59.
2. Abdul-Reda Assiri, *Kuwait's Foreign Policy: City-State in World Politics* (Boulder, CO, Westview Press, 1990), p. 129.
3. Ibid.
4. Robert J. C. Young, 'Postcolonial Remains', *New Literary History*, Vol. 43, No. 1, 2012, p. 33.
5. Ibid, p. 35.
6. Jonathan Crary, *24/7* (London, Verso, 2013), pp. 18–19.
7. Edward W. Said, *Orientalism* (New York, Vintage, 1978), p. 291.

## Fiction's Histories: Marilyn Booth

1. Latifa al-Zayyat, *The Open Door*, translated by Marilyn Booth (Cairo, American University in Cairo Press, 2000). In Arabic: *Al-Bab al-maftuh* (Cairo, al-Maktaba al-injiliziyya al-misriyya,1960).
2. Hassan Daoud, *The Penguin's Song*, translated by Marilyn Booth (San Francisco, City Lights Books, 2014). In Arabic: *Ghina' al-batrik* (Beirut, Dar al-Nahar lil-Nashr, 1998).
3. Zaynab Fawwaz, *Riwayat husn al-'awaqib, aw ghadat al-Zahira* (Cairo, Matba'at Hindiyya, 1899).
4. 'Afifa Karam, *Fatima al-badawiyya* (New York, Maktabat Jaridat al-Huda al-yawmiyya, n.d.).

## What You Don't Read About the Syrian Humanitarian Crisis: Dawn Chatty

1. The *millet* (which comes from the Arabic *milla*, meaning religious community or denomination) was a way of managing the affairs of the Ottoman Empire. All Muslims, whether Shia, Sunni, Alawi or Yezidi, belonged to the Muslim *millet*. Christian and Jewish minority groups of all denominations belonged to separate *millets* and their personal affairs and all family law were managed by the religious hierarchy of their community, not the Ottoman state.

## Defying the Killers: Malu Halasa

1. This name of the poster collective is the one that is widely used. As art curator Charlotte Bank first noted, a more strict transliteration would be 'Al-shaab al-suriyy yarif tariq-hu'.
2. Freehand spray-painting and stencilling were part of a subculture that had been gaining underground popularity in the region. Saudi graffiti critic Rana Jarbou noted that prior to 2011 the two most replicated images across the Arab world were Mickey Mouse and the murdered black American rapper Tupac Shakur (1971–96).
3. Even during his short-lived independent newspaper *Al-Doumari* ('The Lamplighter'), which existed for a little over two years after Hafez al-Assad's son Bashar came to power in 2000, Ferzat still trod carefully. In an issue devoted to corruption, the cartoonist drew transparent IV-bags with fish swimming inside to represent a scandal about out-of-date intravenous serums then still in use in Syrian hospitals.

4. From http://www.englishpen.org/wp-content/
   uploads/2012/04/The-Gist-of-It-Short-Stories-by-
   Rasha-Abbas-Readers-Report-by-Alice-Guthrie.pdf.

5. 'Arters' refers to non-artists using artistic tools and
   techniques. The word derives from 'filmers', as first
   discussed in *Documentary, Witness and Self-Revelation*
   by John Ellis to describe 'those who routinely produce
   video material but without the aim of being a film-
   maker': Zaher Omareen, lecture and presentation, 'A
   Revolution in Syrian Art', British Museum, 20 June
   2014.

6. Sarah Birke, 'How ISIS Rules', *New York Review of
   Books*, Vol. 62, No. 2, 5–18 February 2015, p. 27.

7. The art, photography, film and cartoons featured
   in *Syria Speaks: Art and Culture from the Frontline*
   (London, Saqi Books, 2014) initially appeared in a
   2012–13 touring exhibition, curated by the book's
   editors, which was shown in Europe and the UK. In
   Copenhagen, 39,000 people visited the exhibition
   during Easter week 2013. The exhibition continues to
   tour. In Bradford, it appeared as *Parallel Republic: The
   Art of Civil Disobedience* in 2014. With Syrian graffiti
   artist Ibrahim Fakhri, *Syria Speaks* editors contributed
   an art installation of stencils of Syrian martyrs to the
   *Disobedient Objects* exhibition at the Victoria and
   Albert Musuem in 2014–15, while the British Museum
   is using the book as a guide to begin collecting for a
   new archive of Syrian uprising art.

# CONTRIBUTORS

**Tamim al-Barghouti** is a Palestinian poet, political scientist and columnist. He is the author of *Benign Nationalism: State Building Under Occupation* (2007) and *The Umma and the Dawla: Nation State and the Arab Middle East* (2008). He received a Ph.D. from Boston University and has taught at the American University in Cairo and Georgetown University, Washington, DC. He currently works with the United Nations organisation ESCWA in Beirut. (The views expressed in his essay are the author's and do not necessarily represent the United Nations.) His six poetry collections published in both colloquial and classic Arabic, and his public poetry readings to packed audiences in Palestine, Egypt and elsewhere, have made him one of the most acclaimed Arab poets of his generation. His latest book of poetry is *Ya Masr, Hanet* (*Egypt, It's Close*, 2011).

**James Barr** is the author of *A Line in the Sand: Britain, France and the Struggle That Shaped the Middle East* (2011). Since reading modern history at Oxford he has worked in politics, journalism, finance and diplomacy. He is a visiting fellow at King's College London.

**Marilyn Booth** is the Khalid bin Abdullah Al Saud Professor of the Study of the Contemporary Arab World at the University of Oxford and a Governing Body Fellow at Magdalen College, Oxford. In 2014–15 she was Senior Humanities Research Fellow at New York University, Abu Dhabi, and prior to that held the Iraq Chair in Arabic and Islamic Studies at the University of Edinburgh. Her most recent book is *Classes of Ladies of Cloistered Spaces: Writing Feminist History through Biography in Fin-de-siècle Egypt* (2015). She has translated over a dozen novels, short-story collections and memoirs from the Arabic.

**Dawn Chatty** is University Professor in Anthropology and Forced Migration and the former director of the Refugee Studies Centre, Department of International Development (Queen Elizabeth House), University of Oxford. Her research interests include forced settlement and forced migration, nomadic pastoralism and conservation, gender and development, health, illness and culture, and coping strategies of refugee youth. Among her most recent books are *Children of Palestine: Experiencing Forced Migration in the Middle East* (edited with Gillian Lewando-Hundt, 2005), *Handbook on Nomads in the Middle East and North Africa* (2006) and *Displacement and Dispossession in the Modern Middle East* (2010).

**Selma Dabbagh** is a British Palestinian writer of fiction who lives in London. Born in Scotland, she grew up between Saudi Arabia, England and Kuwait. She has also lived in Bahrain, Egypt, the West Bank and France. Her short stories have been published by Granta, International PEN, Wasafiri and the British Council. Her first novel, *Out of*

*It*, featuring the lives of youth from PLO families returning to Gaza, was published by Bloomsbury in 2011 and was listed as a *Guardian* Book of the Year in 2011 and 2012. Her first radio play, *The Brick*, set in the West Bank and Jerusalem, was produced by BBC Radio 4 in January 2014 and nominated for a 2015 Imison Award. She is currently working on her second novel.

**Khaled Fahmy** is Professor of History at the American University in Cairo. He taught for five years at Princeton University, then for eleven years at New York University, before joining AUC in September 2010. He is currently Arcapita Visiting Professor at Columbia University. His research interests lie in the social and cultural history of modern Egypt. He has published a book on the social history of the Egyptian army in the first half of the nineteenth century (*All the Pasha's Men: Mehmed Ali, His Army and the Making of Modern Egypt*, 1997), a biography on Mehmed Ali (*Mehmed Ali: From Ottoman Governor to Ruler of Egypt*, 2008) and a collection of articles on the history of law and medicine in nineteenth-century Egypt (*The Body and Modernity*, 2004). He is currently finishing a book on the social and cultural history of Egypt in the nineteenth century, as well as editing one on the history of Egyptian law from the Mamluks to the present. Since the outbreak of the 25 January revolution, he has been a regular contributor to local and international media.

**Malu Halasa** is a writer and editor based in London. Her books include *Syria Speaks: Art and Culture from the Frontline* (edited with Zaher Omareen and Nawara Mafoud, 2014), *Transit Tehran: Young Iran and Its Inspirations* (2009) and

*Transit Beirut: New Writing and Images* (2004), *The Secret Life of Syrian Lingerie: Intimacy and Design* (2008), *Kaveh Golestan: Recording the Truth in Iran* (2007) and *Creating Spaces of Freedom: Culture in Defiance* (2002).

**Penny Johnson** is an associate editor of the *Jerusalem Quarterly* (Institute of Palestine Studies). She began working at Birzeit University, Palestine, in 1982 for the university's human rights and prisoners committee and was a founding member of the university's Institute of Women's Studies, writing on Palestinian women, family and social relations in Palestinian society. With Raja Shehadeh, she edited *Seeking Palestine: New Palestinian Writing on Exile and Home* (2013), which won the 2013 Palestine Book Award.

**Justin Marozzi** is a writer and historian. His most recent book, *Baghdad: City of Peace, City of Blood* (2014), won the Royal Society of Literature's Ondaatje Prize in 2015. He is the author of a number of books about the Middle East and Arab world, including a study of the fourteenth-century warlord Tamerlane. For more information, see his website at www.justinmarozzi.com and follow him on Twitter@justinmarozzi.

**Mai al-Nakib** is Associate Professor of English and Comparative Literature at Kuwait University. Her research addresses a wide range of issues linked to cultural politics in the Middle East, from Arab feminism to the ethical question of Palestinians in Kuwait. Her book *The Hidden Light of Objects* (2014) won the Edinburgh International Book Festival's First Book Award in 2014, the first short-story collection to win the award. She is currently writing her first novel.

**Ramita Navai** is an Emmy Award-winning British-Iranian journalist and author. She was the Tehran correspondent for *The Times* from 2003 to 2006. Her first book, *City of Lies: Love, Sex, Death and the Search for Truth in Tehran*, won the Debut Political Book of the Year at the Paddy Power Political Book Awards 2015 and was awarded the Royal Society of Literature's Jerwood Prize for Non-Fiction.

**Alev Scott** was born to a Turkish mother and a British father in London. After studying classics at university, she worked in theatre in London before moving to Istanbul, where she is now based. In 2014 her first book, *Turkish Awakening*, was published by Faber and Faber and was shortlisted for Debut Political Book of the Year. Her writing has appeared in *Newsweek*, the *Guardian*, the *Financial Times* and *The Times*, among other publications. She is currently working on a book tracing the minority communities uprooted during the collapse of the Ottoman Empire.

**Raja Shehadeh** is a writer and lawyer. His books include *Strangers in the House* (2002), *When the Bulbul Stopped Singing: Life in Ramallah Under Siege* (2003), *Palestinian Walks: Notes on a Vanishing Landscape* (2007), for which he won the 2008 Orwell Prize for Political Writing, and *A Rift in Time: Travels with My Ottoman Uncle* (2010). Shehadeh, who lives in Ramallah, is a founder of the pioneering human rights organisation Al Haq, an affiliate of the International Commission of Jurists. His most recent book is *Language of War, Language of Peace: Palestine, Israel and the Search for Justice* (2015).

**Avi Shlaim** is Emeritus Fellow of St Antony's College and Professor of International Relations at the University of Oxford. He is a Fellow of the British Academy. His books include *The Politics of Partition* (1990), *The Iron Wall: Israel and the Arab World* (2000; new expanded edition, 2014), *Lion of Jordan: The Life of King Hussein in War and Peace* (2007) and *Israel and Palestine: Reappraisals, Revisions, Refutations* (2009).

**Salim Tamari** is Professor of Sociology at Birzeit University, Palestine, and editor of *Jerusalem Quarterly* (Institute of Palestine Studies). His book *Year of the Locust* (2011) examines the diaries of First World War soldiers who fought on the Ottoman side and includes his edited translation of the diary of a reluctant Palestinian recruit, Ihsan Turjman. He also co-edited and translated the late-Ottoman and Mandate-era diaries of Jerusalem bon vivant and musician Wasif Jawihariyyeh, published as *The Storyteller of Jerusalem* (2014), which won the 2014 Palestine Book Award.

**Robin Yassin-Kassab** is the author of the novel *The Road to Damascus* (2011). He is a co-editor and regular contributor to PULSE, recently listed by Le Monde Diplomatique as one of its five favourite websites. He is working on a second novel set in the Syrian revolution and has recently contributed to *Syria Speaks* and to *Beta-Life: Short Stories from an A-Life Future*. His journalism on Syria has appeared in the *Guardian*, *National* and *Foreign Policy*, and he has been on radio and television, including the BBC, Channel 4 and al-Jazeera. With Leila al-Shami, he is writing a non-fiction book on the Syrian revolution and counter-revolutions for Pluto Press. His visits to Syria were part of the Zeitouna programme for Syrian refugee children, sponsored by the Karam Foundation.

# ACKNOWLEDGEMENTS

Thanks first to the Edinburgh International Book Festival where our writers initially voiced the perspectives developed in *Shifting Sands* and, above all, to the Festival's engaged audiences, who discuss books and ideas with both passion and civility, creating a vibrant 'republic of letters' in Charlotte Square. Our warmest appreciation to the Festival's (amazingly calm) director, Nick Barley, and to Profile Book's (not always calm) Andrew Franklin, who sat with us in the authors' yurt at the Festival and hatched the idea of this book. The editors also extend their warmest appreciation to the contributors to *Shifting Sands*, who turned their excellent presentations into incisive and lively essays – and all within tight deadlines, meeting every editorial suggestion and query with goodwill and hard work. Thanks also to the team at Profile, particularly Penny Daniel and Lesley Levene, who graciously but firmly steered this book to completion.